MORE

BY

AN OLD CODGER

More Reflective Poems
from
World War 2 to COVID-19
Interspersed with Poems
on
Life under Lockdown

NEIL DAVIES

Published by Independent Publishing Network

Email: info@ipubnet.co.uk

Printed by Print2Demand Limited
1 Newlands Road,
Westoning
Bedfordshire, MK45 5LD

Printed in Great Britain

ISBN 978-1-80068-093-7

Acknowledgement

The publication of this second book of over sixty poems, together with the first book of poems, has only been possible with the help and support of others.

In particular, I must thank Gary of Independent Publishing Network for his advice on matters of publication. Closer to home, my grateful thanks to my son, Russell, (lobsterdm.co.uk) for the design of an excellent website, providing a means of publicising and purchasing my books during lockdown. Not forgetting grandsons Olly Dodd of Wolly Productions for his local support and Ben Tattersall, for 'putting words into my head'!

Finally, thanks to my wife and all my family and friends who have supported me from the start of this late-in-life new experience.

The world-wide pandemic has provided an unusual and unexpected stimulus, with many putting pen to paper, brush to canvas, and words to music. A small bright light in a world of sadness and confusion.

Good friends, good books, and a sleepy conscience:
this is the ideal life.

Mark Twain

Books by the Author:

- POEMS BY AN OLD CODGER

- MORE POEMS BY AN OLD CODGER

A contribution to the social history of recent times and views on modern life.

A man's life is what his thoughts make of it.

Marcus Aurelius

MORE POEMS BY AN OLD CODGER WRITTEN BY NEIL DAVIES

Ben Tattersall

Foreword

With regard to old age, it is said that one's brain becomes better at seeing the entire forest and worse at seeing the leaves. That is the foundation of wisdom.

However, it is a good description of how our memory performs as we grow old.

In later life, a forest of memories of family and friends, of our experiences, our environment, and events, acquired as the brain developed, can be recalled. However, day-to-day memories are like autumn leaves blown aimlessly down to earth.

Each one of us has a life story to tell. However grand, however humble, we can all offer a small piece of the jigsaw of life on this planet at this time. This old codger took advantage of the virus lockdown to turn those parts of his life story that may be of interest to future readers of social history, into poetry.

A new challenge for an old codger.

So many of us have said *'I wish I had asked'*.

Memories are the key not to the past, but to the future.

Corrie ten Boom, Dutch Christian Watchmaker,1892 - 1983

CONTENTS

.

THE MIRACLE OF LIFE

As we witness the miracle of birth,
It is the greatest gift on earth,
A seed that swims to procreate
And life is born as it finds a mate.

With hair and toes and fingers too,
A face with nose, and eyes and ears two,
An early smile but that's just wind,
A heartfelt cry, she's a future Jenny Lind. *

Wrapped up tight, secure, and warm,
The world welcomes this bundle of charm.
Two-way bonding begins in earnest
Fed by bottle or at a mother's breast.

Slowly the child gains strength and stamina,
Sitting, crawling, standing tall, a super star.
And soon this child will be eager to go,
So many interesting sights and sounds to explore.

That planted seed has germinated so well,
A sapling now stands tall creating a spell.
Immature and slender swaying in the wind of life,
But nourished and tended to protect from future strife.

All too soon, this sapling child will move away
To join the forest of human fray,
The miracle of birth is one to behove,
A tree of life from the seed of love.

*1820 - 1887, The Swedish Nightingale (1941 Film)

SEEKING WORK!

It was high summer of 'Forty-Seven',
My friend Frank and I had just reached ten,
Decided to go and seek paid holiday work,
No matter the tasks, we would not shirk.

Two junior school lads with good intent,
We were sure some farmer would relent.
So off we set, to go down the Alyn vale
Some unexpected farmers to regale.

Two large houses hugged the valley wall,
Our Headmaster owned the first, on him we will not call.
No word was spoken, as passing by we tried to slope,
Mr Roberts was to be avoided, but alas, no hope.

"Where are you two lads going?" he asked,
in term-time manner,
From the shrubbery emerged our school commander.
With bold acclaim, we announced our intention,
"Off to find work", our voices now shaking
with rising tension.

We stood there, what will he say, can we get on our way?
"Looking for work, you can work for me today."
He opened his gate and led us into his large garden plot,
We followed with trepidation, as if we were about to be shot.

A well- stocked garden of shrubs and plants and lots of weeds,
This old soldier, gassed in France, deserved our good deeds.
The day grew hotter as we hoed away between the bushes,
His dear old wife came out with tea, we hid our blushes.

At last, we finished our first working day,
What would be our well-earned pay?
As I recall, we received some pennies each, for our efforts,
A day of fresh air, not far to travel, were added benefits.

GROWING UP – THE EARLY DAYS

Life is just a game of snakes and ladders,
The dice of life follows no orders.
The best laid plans are written in sand,
Be prepared; like cards, you're dealt a hand.

It was a very hot Bank Holiday,
Sunny and bright as I made my way
Into a world of grey clouds of fear,
As Europe's crisis was drawing near.

Grey clouds stood over my family too,
Tragedies so raw, sorrow so true.
I guess I was a bright new star
Arriving to heal the deep, deep, scar.

Love and affection for a brand-new life,
To ease the loss, to deflect the strife
Of imminent war and dark, dark days,
Blackout, shelters, bombs, and prayers.

We have been a fortunate generation,
The children of a battered nation.
On its knees but not defeated,
Slowly rebuilding its broken and depleted.

Children of make-do and mend,
Of simple pleasures with little to spend.
Homemade happiness and entertainment,
Of folk welcoming peace and contentment.

Off to school despite the war so intensive,
Went through the gate a little pensive.
Name and peg to hang my coat and hat,
The start of life's phases but know not what.

Village cinema's Saturday matinee was quite a din,
The 'thruppenny rush' as we crowded in.
Hollywood films of Cowboys and Indians fighting
Firing from horseback, always Indians dying.

Pleasures were home-made with little cost,
Communicated with far friends by post.
Span of life in a world out of sight,
Just cinema's Newsreels in black and white.

Generally, boys would always be seen
Wearing short trousers until aged thirteen.
Bruised and scarred knees regularly displayed,
Long length socks, family 'Last' for shoes repaired.

Eleven Plus examination divided the village's homegrown,
Those who remained, those who left for lessons in town.
Friendships lost; friendships made with those elsewhere,
The village youth harmony fractured, difficult to repair.

Those days, Chinese laundered starched white collars,
Shirt studs back and front, looking a million dollars.
'DA' hair style, 'Windsor' tie knot, family 'do's'
Drainpipe trousers, 'winkle picker' shoes.

Church and chapel formal weddings,
Ham salad, black forest gateau, sherry for toasting.
Semi-detached for two grand notes, quite appealing,
Full employment, so apprenticeship from grammar schooling.

In 'Fifty-Three, started work at two pounds a week,
Company training and college day, then later
given a major tweak!
Sponsored on a new three year 'sandwich' college scheme,
Six months at work, six months with my college student team.

October, Nineteen Fifty-Nine, warning note came,
I'm off to play the war-time game.
This was not a planned new direction,
I'm now to be part of the country's military protection!

National Service ended in Nineteen Sixty.
Its intrusion to life and careers such a pity.
But broadened young men into maturity,
New horizons, new friendships, and responsibility.

Be a bush if you can't be a tree,
If you can't be a highway, just be a trail.
If you can't be a sun, be a star,
For it isn't by size that you win or fail,
Be the best of whatever you are.

Martin Luther King, Jnr.

LIFE AT EIGHTY-THREE

I'm still here at eighty-three,
Enjoying a digestive and a cup of tea,
But now all my joints have started stiffening,
And suddenly, I have taken to a bit of sniffling.

I have been around for many years,
Witnessing both happiness and fears.
Eighteen Prime Ministers, this country they have led,
Twelve have worn blue and the rest colour red.

From battery wireless with aerials, valves, and wires,
To digital radios, and many satellite providers
Carrying multiple channels of entertainment and news,
The media taking advantage to expound their biased views.

My hearing is not what it was, you see,
But I know when commentators forget their 't',
Pronunciation no longer prevails, rushed talk, in a dash,
No clarity, no diction, just mumbling hash.

Background 'music' dominates speech so much
I need subtitles, so distracting, but a necessary crutch.
I know it's not earwax, but my hearing will tire,
I hope this life-long faculty does not expire.

My clothes hanging in the bedroom wardrobe,
Now hang on me like an old wet bathrobe.
Time to make a bold decision,
Change the lot or face derision.

My bus pass is no use to me,
Buses no longer run from A to B.
They used to pass quite frequently,
No doubt, they've all been sent across the sea.

But I'm still here, I have no fear
Of mutations of this biblical augury,
I'll do as I'm told and stay safe, you see,
With another digestive and a cup of tea.

WHO WOULD HAVE BELIEVED IT?

Who would have believed it?
Or even given credit,
That in the world we now live,
Change would now be quite so massive.

Supermarket trolleys like perambulators,
Personal details sold to advertising takers.
Year-long choice of all fruit and veg,
A plastic cup and a plastic peg!

Fitted carpets, double glazing
Solar Panels brightly blazing
Dental floss, body potions all 'unique.'
Hot tubs, showers, and bedrooms all en-suite.

Telephone on our wristwatch with location markers,
Kitchens fitted with plumbed dishwashers,
Microwaves, food mixers, all automatic,
Lawn mowers remotely controlled, owners' static.

Digitally enhanced singing and music played,
Photographs discreetly improved and then displayed.
Theatre in your lounge, sitting at ease,
No-one around to cough or sneeze.

A new language is now all around,
It's not foreign, it's world-wide bound.
We old codgers need to get a grip
If we all want to look rather 'Hip.'

Hi-fi, wi-fi, Google, and Zoom
Snapchat, i-pad, it's the internet boom
Email, voice mail, i-phone, too
Spotify, YouTube, to name a few.

Botox, liposuction, by back street hack,
Lips distorted; face skin pulled right back.
Enhancements made to all and sundry,
And they each look like a walking 'Barbie.'

Cars with fatigue-free heated seats and massage too,
Self-cleaning windows, speed control, it parks for you.
Cameras that see all around your car,
Anti-roll bars, so safety wherever you are.

Men working in space for months on end,
Trips around the moon if you have money to spend.
Benefit of knowledge, understanding of this new frontier,
Let us all hope it will enhance life back down here.

For some of us, with this technical rate of change,
It's beyond comprehension, belief, for our mental range.
Codgers like me have witnessed this majestic technical age,
Fascinating, challenging, for history yet another page.

Oh! and now we have a world-wide pandemic!!

THE SECOND BATTLE OF BRITAIN

We are witnessing a second Battle of Britain
The enemy has crossed the channel intent to slain.
Our fighting squadrons rise up, day and night,
To defend us all as they take up the fight.

Our wards and theatres are the battle ground,
Muffled orders, nodded signals, bleeping sounds.
Incessant demand as the toll increases,
But our troops stay firm, not go to pieces.

Like fighter pilots, kitted out, in their flying formation,
In gowns and masks dressed for self-protection,
They toil and sweat, climb high, sink low,
there's no selection,
As this virus mutates and circulates in its
thrust of infection.

Command H/Q records the battle as the days pass by,
Shops 'bombed', pubs and entertainment all now locked.
Strategic plans, regular updates, and we all try
To follow the code, stay home; face to face is sadly blocked.

A different field of human conflict from Churchill's day,
Medals and awards will not be enough for those on low pay.
But we will, again, owe so much to our fighting NHS troops.
Reward them fair and true and with no bureaucratic hoops.

We should hold a final celebration,
Right across a united nation,
To all health and care workers
we will salute you,
at attention.

Many memorials across our land
will mark this current event,
To ease the loss of those who
to their heavens have been sent.

MY COUSIN AND I

Lord Beveridge's welfare report in Forty-Two,
And it was time for me to report for school.
The Liverpool blitz had come to an end
And their bombers that flew over us; a 'godsend'.

My nearby cousin in a higher year,
Kept an eye on me from her playground near.
She was akin to an older sister in those troubled days,
But a mixed blessing in a number of ways.

Wherever she went I tagged along,
Wednesday evening it was a prayer and a song.
Band of Hope at the Glan Aber chapel, spotlessly clean,
Praying and singing "Jesus wants me for a sunbeam".

On Mondays, it was girls' Red Cross training.
Surrounded by eager lasses' keen on bandaging,
Wrapping me up like a scared trussed bird.
I really must have appeared quite absurd.

Come Sundays it was Sunday school,
To agree I was a fool.
Held across the valley at the nearer village church,
I was always left in an unpleasant lurch.

Waiting for my older dear cousin's later ending,
I stood alone, class dismissed, my presence sending
A message to the other village lads released,
Who forgot about Christianity and any promised peace.

Tormented and teased as one from across the valley,
I waited patiently at the gate, no one was 'pally'.
Outnumbered, I suffered in silence,
Until the seniors revealed their presence.

One pleasure I still remember, the place, the scene,
My cousin had collected each 'Sunny Stories' magazine.
We cycled to a children's home near-by,
The delight on their faces near made me cry.

At Christmas, we always decorated our room for free,
Homemade chains, a holly branch for a Christmas tree.
Those childhood memories have stayed with me,
A grounding, I guess, for what was to be.

CHARITY

Old Northern advice: -
"Don't do owt for nowt,
Unless thee're doing it for thee sen."
and
"Tha dun't get summat for nowt"

My home, a new mining village,
Attracting miners from far and wide,
Mixing tradition, religion, and heritage,
Which was held onto with fervent pride.

This Yorkshire piece of questionable advice,
Uncharitable sentiment may not be nice,
Displayed on plates and mugs like china tomes
Reflecting life's struggles in Northern homes.

Today, so many charities have been created
Filling gaps where needs must be placated.
Volunteers, both young and old, offer their skills,
Their time, their service, with lower staffing bills!

There are 170,000 charities in this country
Supported by sixty four percent of us who volunteer,
The second highest nation giving to charity,
With two million food banks for all our needy.

This expanding benevolence of individuals,
commerce, and industry,
Such tangible benefaction for all to see.
It's true love towards one's fellow man in distress
And to all creatures living in wretchedness.

IT DOES NOT HAPPEN BY ITSELF!

Don't put it down, put it away,
Don't leave it there, do as I say.
Those things in the floor won't wash by themselves,
Or are you expecting a squadron of laundry elves?

Why is the towel trailing the floor?
And your pyjamas hanging on the bathroom door?
Along with your socks, an unsightly pair
And the sink drain is full of your blue bleached hair.

Your shoes are here and there, all over the place
And one of your shoes has lost its lace.
Who are you waiting for to clean your shoes?
It's time to wake up and pay your dues.

Cleanliness is next to godliness, some will say,
Elbow grease is free, otherwise you pay.
I guess these words are familiar to many
Young and old, as we try to live in harmony.

Could it be that we all have too much?
A throw-away lifestyle or one of debauch?
How we work, how we live, what we do,
This country's fighting litter left around by you.

WHEN FANTASY BECOMES REALITY

Having mastered the art of reading,
Children's comics were quite appealing,
Coloured illustrations each with a 'balloon' story,
To allay our wartime fears and worry.

There was ample choice of such reading material,
Beano, Dandy, Hotspur, Wizard, the Girl Annual,
Printed on wartime paper, sold at two old pennies,
To counteract the German propaganda stories.

My early choice was the Radio Fun's juvenile rag.
The media stars, each one a comic lag,
Depicted in print in many amusing situations,
Then swap it with my friends or relations.

A new larger comic was created, 1950 was the date,
The Eagle arrived to 'entertain and educate'.
From aircraft of the future, to travelling in space,
*Dan Dare, Pilot of the Future, what an ace!

Twenty pages, eight in colour, on quality paper,
Battles in the air, the sea, for me to savour.
Invasions of space men and bugs, scientific facts projected,
Dan fighting them off or flying to planets to be protected.

The Eagle was the idea of a clergyman with a desire,
Reverend Marcus Morris from Southport, Lancashire,
Based the comic and annuals on Christian values
Disillusioned with children's books and annuals.

His diligent illustrator, Frank Hampson, had great foresight,
On space craft, space travel and future flight.
Headgear so close to what our fighter pilots wear today,
A successful comic until Morris lost control
of content and say.

Now space ventures are beginning to stack,
Men and women are flying off this planet and back,
A man in a flying suit has crossed the channel,
Those comic illustrations were no flannel.

I feel privileged to have lived to see those comic book ideas
Become reality across the span of over seventy years.
Making comparison with today's aeronautical
and space production,
And our future flying concepts being developed
to construction.

*See inside back cover

MY BLACKSMITH DAYS

I was well into my engineering apprenticeship,
Making switchgear for many a ship,
Power stations, Bradwell and others,
A well organised scheme, working like brothers.

Sadly, the blacksmith died quite suddenly,
A stand-in blacksmith was needed, that was me.
The smithy was not in use for any four-legged beast
More, a multi-purpose workshop, at least.

The blacksmith's hearth heated up one's lunch,
More than iron or steel, sometimes brunch,
The odd bend or twist of a long copper strip,
Needs some heat at the mark and a very firm grip.

Various annealing tanks stood all around,
A case-hardening tank took centre ground.
This tank of hot cyanide was a real threat,
Protective clothing, helmet, and always a sweat.

There was a regular need to fire this tank up
To harden knobs each shaped like an inverted cup.
Into a 'deep fry' basket, a metal strainer,
Lowered by chain into the hot liquid retainer

If any drop of machine shop fluid remained,
As the basket entered the waiting red hot pot
Knobs flew out like bullets and down they rained
On me in my protective suit, so hot.

A new blacksmith was recruited,
For this work he was not suited.
A small chap, a true blacksmith gent,
Spent his life with horses for every military event.

He looked aghast at the tools in neglect
And set about making his own personal set.
When cyanide case hardening jobs arrived,
I was called, he would take cover and hide.

As we sat down to eat our lunch-time meal,
His daily John West tin of fish, for real,
He would offer me advice, a sort of crutch,
"Never let them know you know so much!"
(Or words to that effect)

LOCKDOWN FOR ME

I'm stuck at home
Nowhere to roam,
I pace round and round
My TV is the only sound.

I'll be going crazy very soon
I saw a face in last night's moon.
This lockdown has gone on so long
I'll hug anyone who comes along.

I confess I'm living quite well,
Trapped in my little brick shell,
Our online shopping is coming along,
Some 'unavailable', some I get wrong.

My laptop curser is very delicate
No need to click or touch the plate.
I'm regularly surprised at what I've ordered,
Ten tins of soup, three loaves of bread.

All wiped down when they arrive,
We do all this to keep alive.
Then the apples taste quite queer
But not the wine, nor the beer.

My wife and I are under a strain,
One has indigestion, the other back pain
We need to walk, to shop, to greet,
To amble around a shopping street.

Alas, it's clear whilst this lockdown ran,
Retail shops have hit the pan.
My on-line shopping is here to stay,
A computer course? I'll have to pay.

ADVICE I WAS GIVEN

"Never be as accurate as possible,
But as inaccurate as permissible"

So advised our Design lecturer at college,
As we students were gaining 'the knowledge'.
It referred to tolerances placed on a dimension,
Too limiting – it's costly, wastage,
increases operator's tension.

But this advice applies to life,
Not to be too hard on oneself, creating strife,
Setting standards too high or not necessary,
Or laws that cannot be policed, be wary.

Whilst we strive to do things well,
To make, maintain, to perform, to sell,
Perfection is never a reachable state,
Just accept what is on your plate.

Just take what life throws at you,
Don't expect to be at the front of the queue.
Life is full of new opportunities, so keep alert,
And be prepared your ability to assert.

'Permissible' is allowable, acceptable, legit,
It's not pushing boundaries of decency and wit.
Take care in what you do and what you say,
Or loss of freedom is what you will have to pay.

Just store this advice that I was given,
Balance your life, your work, avoid being driven,
Turn away, never try to get even,
Don't make your life a miserable burden.

MY LIFE-TIME TRANSPORT

A green Hercules bicycle with a dropped handlebar,
All shiny and new, was my first pair of wheels.
A knitted zipped jumper, cycles adorned, I felt like a star,
I am sure many will know just how it feels.

To pay for the cycle a paper round was needed,
I took up a round covering parts of the village sprawl
And beyond, a challenge I should have heeded,
I cycled miles every morn, no time to crawl.

At the right age, I changed to two-stroke power,
BSA Bantam Super, 175 cc, all in red,
It took me to work, in sun, wind, and shower,
And when I went courting, enough said.

It is not easy to chat when the lass is behind,
Action was needed to sit side by side.
So, seeking to please and hopefully be kind,
I bought an old Bond three-wheeler with pride.

This machine had seen better days I fear,
The plastic windscreen was no longer clear.
Sitting six inches from the tarmac on a wooden bench,
Dazzled at night by oncoming cars; rain, I got drenched.

One Saturday noon arrived at my girlfriend's home,
She came down her path; wow! she was so awesome,
Stepped into the love machine, a beauty in all detail,
I pulled the kick start lever by my side but to no avail.

I tried and tried and flooded the engine so much,
This 197 cc Villiers two stroke in an aluminium 'crush'.
Things were looking bad; she sighed; I needed a crutch,
The boys in the street got behind and gave it a push.

Sunday noon I arrived at her home, clean seat, and floor.
"She's gone on the bus," shouted her mother from the door.
Public transport had robbed me of seeing my angel step inside
My mustard Bond love machine, I could have cried.

I sold the Bond at a profit, it was all rather tense,
It was later I returned to motoring and life-long expense.
I am off to join the RAF on Her Majesty's Service duty.
Need a driving license so I can buy a second-hand beauty.

It was '61, and near our apartment Ford cars were sold,
Their sales were strong, the showroom bright; they were bold.
A marketing ploy, a unique driving school at their showroom.
Nine lessons on the road, and three in their upstairs classroom.

Sixty years or so, when driving was a pleasure to go
Far and wide as travelling along was reasonably slow.
Hand signals through the lowered window
to indicate your intention,
Bayonet light bulbs, starting handles,
no belt for one's protection.

I passed my test and bought a car of some age and wear,
Nightly drain of radiator, eggs don't work, as some do swear,
A Ford Anglia with a leaking radiator and steering problem,
This old bus did us well until we had to change our stratagem.

Our first-born daughter arrived and was thriving so well,
She rode in a coach-built pram, fine and large, looking swell.
The old Anglia failed the test to accommodate this chariot
To take her places, meet her family, but I'm no idiot!

The answer to our plight was in my sight,
A new Ford Thames van would make things right.
VAT free and based on the new Anglia car front end,
The pram fitted in like a glove, nothing to remove nor bend.

But here is the twist – a design fault I exposed,
This hybrid unit was not as the adverts posed,
Like 'cut and paste' in lazy letters makes me rage,
A starting handle but no hole in bumper to engage!

Several cars later and car density now so great,
Pollution, exhausts with four pollutants to irritate,
Poor air quality, noise, congestion, climate change
Must be addressed, it's a world-wide challenge!

I heeded the call to protect the planet from burning gases,
I compromised and bought a used hybrid Auris
And do my bit to save the planet in my latter years.
Fuelled infrequently, motoring accountants shedding tears.

I have concerns about electric cars and charging,
Streets littered with charging 'furniture', so unpleasing,
Many cars are left roadside or driveway overnight,
House fronts littered with electric cabling, day, and night.

Carparks full of these erect charging points, for all to see,
No space to park, nor to wait for a point to become free.

Will these cars be beyond the common man from the start?
Or just for those with big purses treating cars like art.
Many ideas and many ideals have fallen apart,
The whole here is greater than the sum of its parts. *

* With apologies to Aristotle

SPRING EQUINOX DAY

It's March and the day is dawning.
The blackbird is back and calling.
His medley of songs to enthral,
To greet the day and thrill us all.

He sits high upon an urban 'tree',
On our TV aerial for all to see.
Another bird calls back across the street,
This exchange of dialogue is not discrete.

Another year at our Equinox day,
This pink beaked bird is having his say
At four o'clock on a cold bleak morn,
Now I know that Spring is born.

Today the blackbird is seeking a wife,
Together to start a parallel life.
These songbirds all know the score,
It's a wonderful form of musical semaphore.

This blackbird and mate will soon be flying about,
Active in a border bush, a nest no doubt.
Tread careful now, must not disturb,
Oh! Nature is quite superb.

Early evening, his recital he again performs,
Tweeting, rolling, trilling, in almost human forms.
But he must take care of his exposure,
Felines about, threatening his brief life's closure.

A battalion of sparrows in opposition,
Chattering away in their hidden position.
A sparrow hawk now making regular visits,
Feathers and bones scattered about in bits.

Pigeons and gulls making an unruly commotion,
All this in our quiet urban conurbation.
Cooing and screaming in disharmony,
They really should be out by the sea.

Listen, do not talk, sit under a tree,
Nature's innocents for all to hear, it's free.
What better way to lift every heart?
For this virus, they are all playing their part.

EDUCATION FOR THE FUTURE

"He who can does, he who cannot, teaches"
Wrote G B Shaw as he denigrated teachers.

Not everyone can teach,
Not everyone can preach.
Imparting knowledge is an art,
Control, attention, from the start.

What is the future role of education?
To establish the pillars of life for every nation.
Organisation of mind and being, for every soul,
To live in comfort, peace, and self-control.

Computers can now offer facts and data,
Even how to cook a sweet batata*
It's developing imagination, innovation,
Invention, illustration, and application,
That must be taught to our future nation
Supported by sound communication.

To search forward and not look back
And live a life following the right track.
To balance a level of personal revenue with needs
And our obligations and responsibilities.

History of life, of actions in times long ago
Must be seen in context not by the modern status quo.
Glorified stories belie the truthful actions
And serve no purpose, just create unpleasant reactions.

The approach to teaching must be of a different kind,
Students encouraged to develop an open mind.
The emphasis changing from learning facts and equations
To applying the data to extend their imagination.

Learning environment to support open minds,
Flexible space to encourage innovation of all kinds.
Looser control of past rigid thought,
New approaches by staff, not as I was taught.

*Sweet potato

POST-TRAUMATIC STRESS DISORDER

Military conflicts in years gone by
On land or sea or in the sky,
Approached in line abreast, colours held high,
Uniforms worn and battle cries.

The enemy was clear for all to see,
As comrades advanced, no doubt in fear.
A level of stress as battles abound,
Dead and injured lying all around.

Modern conflicts are more insidious affairs,
The unseen enemy creates fear and nervous flairs.
Casual dress, hidden armaments, just passers-by,
Men, women, and children primed to die.

From death at the front, to death in the street,
Death at the corner, death at your feet.
The stress is unbearable, affecting your sleep,
Grown men, and boys, with memories, they weep.

Another dimension to this traumatic stress,
Are wives and mothers, for news they press.
Their stress is different, it is the unknown,
As they sit by the fire, worried, and all alone.

P T S D is a conflict within oneself,
They all lie on that trauma shelf.
Flashbacks, nightmares, anxiety,
Support is needed, not expressions of pious pity.

Will wars ever cease, with peace worldwide?
Cordite, bullets, and tanks thrown aside.
Can man ever live in harmony with each other?
Human losses we will no longer savour.

Nations must be wary of those cyber wise,
Systems infected; countries paralysed.
Not one shot fired, a different stress,
Invisible enemies but danger no less.

Will wars be a thing of the past?
Or will there be an almighty blast?
Let us have peace along every border,
No more Post Traumatic Stress Disorder.

WOMEN THROUGH THE AGES

"Put four old men around four pints of beer
And they'll talk more about work than they do in a year.
Put four old women around four cups of tea
And they'll talk more about scandal than ever you see."

This old adage may reflect the past,
When every man possessed an iron Shoe Last,
And women's lives were centred on their street,
Spending hours scrubbing floors and maintaining the heat.

It reflects the time of selfish male domination,
When fathers always ate on their own, an abomination,
And women were made to feel quite small
By men who needed to appear big and tall.

Women's horizons were narrow and flat,
Fall in love and that was that.
Wasted talents and a frustrated life,
Trapped indoors with the title 'Housewife.'

But women are multiskilled and clever,
Running a home, a mother, and carer.
Forward planning is a constant skill,
And they have a solution to every ill.

The old adage reflects one thing,
A woman is a social human being,
Seeking interactive communication,
A skill that's needed in every nation.

Some men may discuss their jobs
and how hard they work
But is it a case of 'talk the talk'
not 'walk the talk',
Defending the male status quo
and protecting oneself.
Promoted to a position too high
up the shelf.

It has taken years of hunger and strife,
As the Establishment maintained
the old male life.
But persistence and example have won the day,
Women's talents and ability have come into play.

Now all are equal, and things should change,
Women have the opportunity across the range.
Appointments must go to the best of the sheaf
No matter what gender, culture, or their belief.

A YEAR OF COVID-19

Sadly, I've become a little flat,
No-one is around, no-one to chat.
Netflix, iPlayer, hub, and My5,
Help keep my wife and I remain alive.

We've zoomed to chat on our agreed slot,
Our shopping now is all on-line,
A slip of the finger and I've bought the lot,
I'll have to send some back, but not the wine!

What's the point of ironing the wash?
Or trimming one's beard and old moustache
Total lockdown, nowhere to go
Just keep trimming each fingernail and toe.

My laptop and printer have fallen out,
I have no-one now I can shout,
And my printer's forgotten it's a scanner,
It's no use looking for a spanner.

I've cleared my garden of leaves as they fell,
All stored in my leaf mould box so well.
A pack of worms arrived in the post,
I've introduced them to their dying host.

Our sixtieth married Christmas together,
Having endured COVID-19 and the weather.
This Diamond year has been no fun,
Housebound through both rain and sun.

No summer party for all our guests,
No masked ball, just masks, at the PM's behest.
Washing our hands and all things touched by man,
For this epidemic, they had no plan.

But we have carried on together,
With all our memories of years gone by.
So many places spent with sunny weather,
Happy to venture by road, rail and even fly.

Of excited Christmas mornings,
The children full of glee
As they emptied their bedside stockings,
And presents around the tree.

The shepherds and wise men travelled
To see the child, the old Book's story unravelled.
We used the world-wide web, we could not go
To see our new family addition, she's all aglow.

Watches and clocks went back again,
It really has become a pain.
We *'Spring Forward'* and then *'Fall Back'*,
My poor body clock is being racked.

This annual time change may soon lose its effect
When to work from home we'll all elect.
Empty shops and empty towns,
'Brown sites' for Amazon's landing grounds.

I'll take my jab without a wince,
It's been a long time since
We held, kissed, and sat down with a brew,
And poured out tea in more cups than two.

It's time to stop looking over our shoulder
And face a new world, strong and bolder.
Recovery will be a greater challenge to us all,
Another era with our backs against the wall.

There was a very cautious man
Who never romped nor played.
He never laughed or ever dreamed
Nor kissed a pretty maid.
So when he passed away they say,
Insurance was denied.
For since he never really lived
They claim he never died.

Anonymous (one variation)

FOOTBALL AND TEAMWORK

Saturday afternoon's game of footballing attrition,
Teams on the pitch and in position,
Referee checks around, recognising his obligation,
Keeping a smooth flowing game is his intention.

The whistle blown, the game is on,
A derby match, will it be a friendly one?
The home side is facing a lowering sun,
Second half the opposition has a setting one.

A close fought match with two fit teams,
A no-score draw to come it seems.
The home side crowd are at full voice,
Manager's dilemma, time for a substitute choice?

The opposition is staying tight and pressing
Keeping our half-back line guessing.
A tackle is made, the referee looks for a flag,
No foul, our lad's away, he's no lag.

From the left he sends the ball across the dipping sun
Met by his colleague on a fast, wing run.
The defence, flat footed, pulling back,
Our sharp runner lobs the ball into the centre pack.

Up goes the striker, ball back of the net,
Now this is where I get upset.
The scorer running around like a demented Panto dame
Stripped to the waist, waving his shirt, claiming fame.

But let's be clear, ball in the net, keeper to gather,
Created by team members all working together.
The one at the end gets all the recorded glory,
But I see it as a different story.

Its teamwork that achieved that winning goal,
Players, coach, and backroom staff all.
Its teamwork that succeeds in any challenging situation,
Its teamwork we need now across our infected nation.

AN OBSERVATION ON OUR RAILWAYS

When steam railways arrived, it was no stunt,
A man was appointed to walk in front.
The ride was at a very slow pace,
Carrying bowtie men, ladies in satin and lace.

An engineering dragon blowing out steam,
For Trevithick the culmination of his dream.
Two hundred years ago on Saint Valentine's Day,
A wager was laid to pull a load along the Merthyr Way.

From Penydaren to Abercynan, ten ton of iron
And seventy men, were pulled and the bet was won.
From this small beginning rail transport was born,
Rail services now left horse and barge both forlorn.

The Great Western line ran along the Alyn valley slope,
As a boy I climbed a tree alongside the track waiting in hope
For a Castle class engine, curved side pipes, passing along,
A County class, straight pipes, appeared, having waited long.

From those sliding, turning, hissing parts,
Each a dramatic work of engineering art.
As black coal was shovelled by man,
Into a red-hot furnace, the stoker with a red-faced tan.

As coal was damned and pits closed down,
Came engines powered by diesel oil, acrid and brown.
Polluting the air, one's nose, the ground,
Creating a dull different engine sound.

No visible moving part,
Smooth, sleek, modern technical art.
Along came electric motors run from the grid,
Now to the fore, silently, a form of industrial hybrid.

This brief review now brings me to
High speed travel for me and you.
Two hundred and fifty miles per hour on HS2,
The countryside it's trouncing all the way through.

Just to reduce our journey time
By a perfectly straight railway line.
No curves, no humps, right through the hills,
Clearing the land so no wet leaves causing spills.

From five miles per hour and a man with his flag,
To a train going so fast and with no seat belt nor airbag.
A blur of the countryside for those inside,
A blur of a passing train for those standing at the trackside.

Do we need to reduce our journey time?
Do we need to travel on a railway line?
Do we need to travel for work at speed at all?
Zooming in seconds will be the call.

LENIN'S ADVICE

*Capture the cinema, and you capture
the hearts and minds of the people.*
Lenin (1870 – 1924)

Lenin's revolutionary thought, here in writing,
Is now more worrying and disturbing.
For cinema, read modern visual screening,
Right in the home and where you are working.

Persuasive content, attractive offers, and seduction,
Misleading, lies, and creating digital media addiction.
For our vulnerable young and old
Control of content must be bold.

Hearts and minds need protection,
Tighter regulation of production
And the media's programme selection.
Standards set that meet fitness and approbation.

Fitness for purpose, fitness for viewing
All programme content through day and the evening.
Our 'cinema' now is so readily on-line
It's constantly available anywhere, anytime,

The danger of capture is infiltration,
A threat to the security of every nation.
A mammoth task for cyber police to pursue
And stop the actions of every evil cyber guru.

OUR MILKMAN

I'm eighty-three and feeling good,
My wife cooks me nutritious food.
The odd itch and a stiffening joint,
But I can bend, and I can point.

Some years ago, our shopping was a pain
Laden trolleys, four wheels moving quite insane.
So, Home Delivery for heavy goods was booked,
Grab a slot, choose your goods, we were hooked.

A morning milkman came near each day
So, ordered two bottles daily, with monthly pay.
No more plastic, milk to the door,
Delivered early, even when the rain doth pour.

Through all weathers, delivery is sound
And fresh eggs from local farms around.
Lockdown came, prompt Home Deliveries stalled,
But our milkman's dairy had it solved.

Butter, bread, eggs, and cream,
Bacon, crumpets, yogurts, a full team.
It met our needs, brought to the door,
As lockdown weeks became more and more.

It's folk like this with a human touch,
Maintain their service and never slouch
When all around life is falling flat,
Our milkman is always happy to have a chat.

Raise your glass to those who serve,
Police and Fire, each one needing
a very strong nerve,
Bin men, Post men and women too,
All stand tall and proud, for we salute you.

TV - THEN AND NOW

Logie Baird's first TV outside broadcast in Thirty-One,
Showed viewers how The Derby race was won,
Television has grown from that early day,
First with valves, wires, and tubes of cathode ray.

CRT projector gun, enclosed, never seen,
Fired electrons to excite the particles on the screen.
Offering programmes in black and white
Taken up by the BBC, setting families' desires alight.

In the 'fifties as workers' pay increased,
Electrical goods were bought or leased.
TV rental offered a way to view,
H or X shaped aerials fitted aloft by the company crew.

Housed in cabinets to match the décor,
Hidden away until you opened the door.
These bulky units grew more grand
As the TV screens began to expand.

Nine-inch, fourteen-inch, and bigger still,
Until the TV stood proud, the room to fill.
Then came LCDs, LEDs, and plasma screens,
And Slimline TVs due to OLEDs.

I recall those early days of anticipation,
Watching Saturday football with elation.
A family member invited me to join and watch
The rounds of the Amateur Cup, every match.

It was decided we should rent a TV set,
Adorn our living room with its curtains of net.
Broadcasting was not continuous then,
Ending with the National Anthem at Ten.

'Andy Pandy' for the young viewers each morn,
'Pebble Mill at One' of magazine form.
'What's My Line', for evening viewing,
Interludes set within the nightly programming.

I remember, still, that family evening after tea,
Father, mother, sister, and me,
Settled down to enjoy our new rental TV,
Programmes that we loved to see.

As we watched this popular show,
The wall behind began to glow,
Brighter and brighter and flickering so,
This was not how things should go.

The TV set was now on fire,
A sort of indoor domestic pyre.
Father pulled out the plug so bolden,
Lifted the set and took it out into the garden.

My father did not even pause,
The 'post-mortem' identified the cause,
Some Transformer had over-heated.
Our television set now depleted.

Our hero took it in his stride,
My mother looking on with pride.
Village pit power supply would frequently vary
As demand increased, things often got quite scary!

COAL MINERS' LIVES - 1

Growing up, I was made aware *
What my mining grandfathers had to bear,
Walk to work a mile or three or more
Then walk the same, or crawl, and start to bore.

Miners had to watch their words, maintain their pride,
Chapel deacons, Sunday school teachers, working side by side
Hewing coal and humour shared,
Chapel hymns by Chapel choirs, voices paired.

Ladies' bloomers from the market stall,
A dual purpose for miners all
To tolerate the fiery heat down each deep, deep, seam,
To wear in the baths, certain parts should not be seen!

When miners work boots fell apart,
Village cobblers carved a wooden second start.
These clogs echoed around every empty morning street,
Holes punched out to drain sweat from socks and feet.

As they waited for the three - level cage to descend,
Singing voices then rising as up as they ascend.
Hymns and arias ringing throughout the showers,
A solo voice prompting tenors and basses of the local choirs.

An injured man or one deceased,
Straight home by pit horse and cart, life released.
Cleaned at home, laid out, and now at peace,
Whip-round coins offered for family's financial ease.

They took this job with its constant fear of instant death,
Overbearing heat and dust-filled breath.
No pension scheme, no holiday pay, no holidays,
No NHS, no social care, just one to lead the family prayers.

Let us all recognise those miners' strength,
Facing danger every shift of mammoth length,
Helped by friendship, trust, and loyalty,
Comforted by singing together in vocal harmony.

*Accounts from my mother

COAL MINERS' LIVES - 2

When mines were privately owned
And the life of seams below not known,
No guarantee of regular weekly wages,
Sometimes, no guarantee of work for ages.

At the crack of dawn miners stood like sheep,
Seeking the call to go down deep.
'No work today, come back tomorrow',
Families left to beg or borrow.

The owners were a crooked bunch,
Enjoying a daily hot cooked lunch,
While men and boys toiled deep below,
'Snapping tin' of bread and H_2O

The owners picked their 'Charter Masters',
To hack the coalface, praying for no disasters,
'Butty Men' who chose their working teams
Hoping to reveal good quality coal seams.

What was shovelled and sent up to the top
From the dark, damp burrow with its wooden prop.
The owners would then decide the grade
And how much the Butty Man would be paid.

Was the grade ever correctly called?
The scales set fair or discretely mauled?
The 'Butty Men' received their pile of money,
The workers lining up, cap in hand, given pennies.

This state of play came to an end with World War Two,
The mines came under Government control in 'Forty-Two.
The huge demand for coal came into play
And the industry moved on to 'Vesting Day'.

In Forty-Seven the mines were nationalised, that January,
Managed 'on behalf of the people' by the NCB.
Almost a thousand collieries and every asset,
Taken up and placed in the NCB basket.

After the war, working men's pay was weekly,
Five-pound cash in hand, not banked monthly.
Easier to budget by controlled outlay,
Not those escalating monthly debts to repay.

But cash in hand presented many a curse
Before it reached the dear wife's purse.
Pubs were built close to pit-head ground,
As were bookmakers' runners all around.

Men fell afoul of these addictive temptations, so heartless,
Hard-earned money was lost or wasted, due to weakness.
Dreams of quick-rich lifestyle never to be,
Could not even afford a week's holiday by the sea.

Things moved on from pay packets by hand,
To banking and cheque books, oh! so grand.
Then on-line banking, cards to swipe and go.
Our cashless age: for the Royal Mint it will be a blow.

Copper and silver weighed down our garments,
But they sufficed when making payments.
Then paper notes, many becoming grubby and creased,
The cost of living meant their numbers increased.

Miners' pay reflected the annual rate of inflation
Over the years across our nation,
Their life and living, a mirror of so many similar
Conditions that others would find familiar.

In between yesterday's regret and tomorrow's dream

is today's opportunity, seize the chance

Ifeanyi Enoch Onuoha

POLITICS

It's election time for the devolved UK assemblies,
The candidates' leaflets are full of pleas.
"Vote for me and I will right all wrongs",
Wonderful things will happen, are their promising songs.

These 'Conference League' hopefuls dressed in party hues,
Fail to note the income comes from tax-payers' dues.
The pot is not an overflowing bowl of gold,
It is so silly to be so bold.

An opportunity has arisen
For those who talk with derision,
Of our United Kingdom's fate,
And seek separation handed on a plate.

Many in their clan patterned kilts across the border,
Need to be reminded and brought to order.
The Jacobite rising and Bonny Prince Charlie
Triggered our British National Anthem, you see.

A patriotic song of 1745 took hold,
Became the National Anthem we sing so bold.
The Anthem is five verses long, to pray
For the safety of the Monarch of the day.

We lazy people just sing verse one,
Sometimes the first and third are sung.
Hymns Ancient & Modern, number 577, has three,
But verse two is the one for me.

I quote-:
O Lord our God arise,
Scatter her(his) enemies
And make them fall;
Confound their politics,
Frustrate their knavish tricks,
On thee our hopes we fix,
God save us all!

So apt today as long ago,
These candidates just need to know
Enough is enough of the anti-status quo,
And the behaviour that has gone on before.

It's a firefighting task all the way,
If your party, in power, can stay.
Be honest, ignore the criticising Joes,
Be true, there will be challenging highs and lows.

CHRISTMAS AT COVID -19 TIME

Christmas starts when Advent is over,
But not according to the media 'Bovver'.
The trendy young at the BBC,
Started Christmas when we
were just back from the sand and sea.

Bombarded with emails you can't unsubscribe
And there is no chance they will take a bribe.
Black Friday is now every day and night,
Installing panic, the queues are stretching out of sight.

Time to off-load old goods and stock,
Their shelf life's over, it's quite a shock.
They shrink or itch; pottery advertised as a 'smasher',
Can't be placed in our new dishwasher.

There's 'no return of goods', so send to charity,
A recent form of transferability.
A Christmas stocking is a sight to see,
Not mum's old tights cut high above the knee.

Houses are lit up with streams of lights,
Could be mistaken by arriving flights
To Runway One for final approach to land,
Air Traffic Control are burying their heads in the sand.

Old Santa, poor chap is having a rant,
Amazon delivers whatever you want.
It's Santa's new commercial enemy,
To the door, not down the chimney!

Good old Christmas music and song,
Abused and belted out all day long
By leading artists now short of a bob or three,
And those craving constant appearance on our TV.

Christmas dinner is an exotic sight,
Every food must be cooked just right.
That's according to our many expert cooks,
But my wife does not need to read their books.

Let us keep it simple this Christmas time
And think of all those folk infected and died,
Of those whose minds have been distorted
By war, alcohol, drugs, or things snorted.

Let us not waste our precious resources,
Cut out obesity, excess, and exotic sauces.
Keep fit and healthy and safe this Christmas tide
For those caring staff and others at the NHS bedside.

FROM THE ORGAN STOOL – 1

Ten years after the end of World War Two,
Appointed church organist, moving from pew to stool.
Two services on Sundays, choir practice each week,
Some Saturday weddings, funerals midweek.

Emotions are high at these two celebrations,
Excitement at one, sorrow at loss of a friend or relation.
Choice of music is personal, if occasionally strange,
Reflecting the popular trend at the time and age.

Whenever I received a personal request,
I would always endeavour to do my best.
From the bride requesting the Benson & Hedges
'advert' music,
To the emotional desire for a famous orchestral classic.

At eighteen, I was just new in the post.
A village boy whose life was about to be lost,
Not even a teenager; he had heard the musical score
Of an opera based on Italian folklore.

Intermezzo from Cavalleria rusticana by Mascagni
Was the boy's request passed on to me,
The church was packed, mourners all,
I practiced this piece and answered the call.

This opera of lost love and retaliation,
A young villager home from a military mission
Finds his fiancée has married another,
Affairs and seduction end in a bloody bother.

Here, a brief life that's lost so soon and tragic,
A heart that will never enjoy love's magic.
A spirit to grow and challenge life,
A home and comfort with children and wife.

Holding back tears, emotions so rife,
At the loss of such a young life.
The funeral service has stayed with me
Whenever I play that music by Pietro Mascagni.

After silence, that which comes nearest
to expressing the inexpressible is music.

Aldous Huxley

FROM THE ORGAN STOOL - 2

Organs come in all shapes and types,
Some for home and some with fake pipes,
Pipe and reed and theatre Wurlitzers
Now, electronic with many sounds and mixers.

My childhood home had just one family room,
But held both piano and organ at one end,
Our 'American Organ' had played many a tune,
Air is sucked through metal reeds, so will not bend.

For clarity, Harmoniums have air blown through,
Organists must pedal as they play, that's true,
Both have pedal operated bellows, to drive the air.
But more, paddles pushed out by knees, the pair.
This increases the volume of sound on its way.
Organists play, pedal, with knees going out sideway!

I mention these facts for one good reason,
Stationed at RAF Cosford, teaching things technical,
The camp had closed for the Christmas season,
So, services held at the adjacent hospital chapel.

I was asked to play for the midnight Eucharist,
A touching experience; converted ward at its best.
A small harmonium stood on the polished floor,
Military floors are polished to perfection and more!

A rousing carol was on the service agenda,
Needing plenty of air to send the sound asunder.
I pedalled hard; my knees well spread,
The sound heard by a patient in a nearby ward bed.

Then slowly my stool started sliding away,
As I pedalled with earnest, so keen to play.
The more I pedalled the further I slid backwards
Away from the keyboard, paddles, pedals, music, words!

Over enthusiasm and fervour never pays,
Just keep a steady pace in all your ways.
Mistakes will occur if you rush in headlong,
From running a mile to singing a song.

FROM THE ORGAN STOOL - 3

This is a story of confusion,
The unexpected due to enthusiasm,
Or was it an act of final goodbye,
To stave off emotion and poised to cry.

In my late teens and village church organist,
My paternal grandfather sadly ceased to exist.
A small man who rarely spoke a word at all,
An old miner with a quiet soul.

Brother, Frank, a stretcher bearer answered the call,
At the 'Front' in WW1 and saw it all.
Both presbyterian, through and through,
All Sankey's hymns they both knew.

Asked to play for my grandad's funeral service,
The chapel organ, a familiar model, in its place.
All was well, mourners seated, service began,
I thought I had the music working to plan,

Voices good and strong as they sang in parts,
The final hymn was sung right from their hearts,
Passion was rising as the last verse was sung.
And as I moved to play 'Amen',
The congregation started the verse again!

Again, they sang the last verse, and again,
When will they stop and sing 'Amen'?
How was I to know how many times,
It was rather like encores at pantomimes.

Always expect the unexpected,
Be prepared to change, to be corrected,
Always appreciate cultures and traditions,
Be sensitive to all feelings and emotions.

FROM THE ORGAN STOOL - 4

Living in a flat in the Wolverhampton conurbation,
Awaiting accommodation in the nearby military station,
Easter was approaching when I espied
An advert for organist as incumbent had retired.

St George's, a striking church with grounds all around,
An organ to enjoy with majestic sound.
Reverend David Wood, often seen on Midland's TV,
Known affectionately everywhere as Father D.

We met in his large vicarage house full of ample furniture,
With young ordinands at community work of a social nature.
It was agreed I would play
For services at the oncoming Palm Sunday.

A new experience, a new instrument for me to play
Little did I know what else, ahead for me, lay.
It's a common experience for clergy and choir together
To sing a festival hymn processing down the aisle
in an invisible tether.

The hymn began and so did the procession,
The choir singing well whilst in walking motion,
Then gradually the church fell silent,
I leaned backwards; no-one was present.

Everyone had gone, left the church,
I cannot hear singing; I'm left in a lurch.
The long procession is touring the grounds,
A kind of 'Beating the Bounds'.

No way of knowing whether I am in or out of step,
What verse, what line, no one to help.
When will they all return to their pews,
Is someone going to give me the news?

Just sit and wait is all I could do
Until the congregation were back in their pew,
Prepared to start a verse all together, voices blended,
But which verse is to be, or has the hymn ended?

Traditional gestures, symbolic rights, going back years,
Today's red carpet is akin to the use of those palm leaves
Strewn on the ground two thousand years ago,
A mark of honour, with those present bending low.

This Grade Two listed church fell afoul of modern life,
Becoming a supermarket in '78, religion so in strife.
Remember, nothing is sacrosanct nor permanent,
We live in an instant world with little or no sentiment.

OF NO FIXED ABODE

Some are born to lead,
Some are happy to be led,
And some, to help those in need,
To care, feed, or help to bed.

Life plays a part in these divisions,
Opportunities, circumstances, situations,
And charters one's destiny,
Or, perhaps, it's fate that holds the key.

Born in Thirty-Seven, in my Nain's bed,
She a widow with tears still shed.
I came along, to bring her joy,
Her healthy grandson, a strapping boy.

My parents lived happily across the valley,
Renting a cottage on Narrow Lane 'alley'.
Paternal uncle, widower, Charles by name,
Called for help, my parents and little me, came.

This step was a step too far, with hindsight,
His cottage was old, damp, and cold,
Stone flag floor and little natural light,
Toilet up on the bank, so old.

Charles was not an easy man, tall,
and of some countenance,
But with a family trait of temper and dominance.
Father, cousin, and Charles around the table,
Had regular heated arguments on matters of the Bible.

Fate took a hand when War broke out,
Father 'On Reserve' to wait for the shout.
Called up, trained, and sent to help Burma's defence,
Mum and I left alone in Dad's uncle's residence.

Left behind to live with a relative stranger,
In an environment not suitable for a little toddler,
Basic facilities of cold water and coal, our board,
Will matters lead us to being of no fixed abode?

Fate stepped in again, Nain's health began to fail,
Had been too much for a lady already frail.
Loss of husband and youngest son to mine disasters
Her cry for help, my mother to come home and nurse her.

Charles pleaded for us not to leave him alone,
But my mother saw her family duty was the call.
We moved to live where I was born,
As the war intensified for one and all.

My Nain, bedridden in her living room
Was happy for me to feed her tea,
And hear me trying to yodel to lift her gloom.
She passed away in '74, a sad sight to see.

My mother became very anxious and downbeat,
Were we to become of no fixed abode, on the street?
The rent and rent book were down in Nain's name.
For this property, many would place a claim.

My father way across the seas fighting for his country,
Must have been distraught, wrapped with anxiety,
Initiating the loss of tenancy of Narrow Lane,
Left my mother now in a state of mental pain.

Sense prevailed and transfer was finally approved,
The family home secure, we were not about to be moved.
This is a lesson for all those who choose to care,
Be mindful of your security, or it can become a nightmare.

THOSE DAYS: THESE DAYS

Once Wales was the land of music and song,
We said 'Hello' and we all got along.
We'd chatter at the gate or the village shop,
The front doorstep or the local bus stop.

We filled the church, we filled the chapel,
At Harvest we each were given a rosy apple.
We all stood tall when the National Anthems were played
And when the Remembrance wreath was laid.

Men doffed their cap or raised their trilby hat
And opened doors for ladies dressed so smart.
We led the world in steel and coal,
Had courage to work down a deep, dark hole.

We stood on a raised ash bank football ground,
To watch and cheer and fill with sound
When our local team was on the field,
Trying to win that coveted League shield.

We didn't abuse players from other lands,
The ref and players all shook hands.
A game of sport, of fitness and skill,
After a week of hard work and no standing still.

We smelt the earth, we tasted the air
And felt the wind blow through our hair.
We witnessed nature in all its glory
Two legged, four legged, and many an aerial story.

We walked and cycled for many miles,
Unbridled views and sights of wonder,
A nod or a wave, exchanging many broad smiles,
Then we piled into cars to go far yonder.

We blocked out the spectra of our land
As we sped along feeling quite grand,
In a shell of steel and power to our feet,
Recumbent in our 'leather' heated seat.

The beauty of Wales was cast aside
As we sought new vistas, we lost our pride.
We scattered our rubbish across the land
In rivers, on hills, in towns, all thrown by hand.

Mountains and valleys and many natural beauties
Vandalised by quads and off-road utilities.
City noise echoes across our hills, far and wide
Along our coast and every beach waterside.

The life and health of any nation
Is dependent on its sanitation,
And trust, respect, and obligation,
Devoid of these, it's an unpleasant situation.

Greatest of all is one of pride
Pride in our towns, cities, and countryside.
Pride in overcoming our nation's many threats,
Pride in one's life, with no regrets.

The birds of our land just keep on singing
High in the sky enjoying their natural flying.
We, too, need to keep on singing
For those with Hiraeth for the land they're missing.

Lockdown has opened our eyes to realise
What we have is a wonderful prize.
Pride is returning in all things Welsh
Our hills and valleys, we're beginning to relish.

FAMILY AND FRIENDSHIP

Into this world you are delivered,
A member of your awaiting kindred.
You cannot escape the family tree,
You are now part of their ancient ancestry.

There is no choice when you arrive,
An innocent babe, in shock but very alive.
The umbilical cord that's cut at birth,
Just a physical break from womb to earth.

Your identity is logged for eternity
Into a specific family community.
That modern birthday card you often see
Reminding the relative *"You're stuck with me!"*

But you will meet many a friend,
Make friendships that will never end.
They too have family trees and ancestry,
Friends with an air of personal mystery.

Thrown together unexpectedly,
At work, at play, or over a cup of tea.
A personality that offers a helpful hand
Or one whose friendship stretches across the land.

A common sharing of friendship together
Strolling through all sorts of personal weather,
A bond of unspoken word, a nod, a smile,
Someone for whom you would walk a mile.

The reward of true friendship that's close and good
Is 'To understand and to be understood'. *
The ancient Greek, Euripides, may have had motives
Uttering *"One loyal friend is worth ten thousand relatives"*!

*Seneca

Beautiful memories are like old friends
They may not always be on your mind,
but they are forever in your hearts.

Susan Gale

MY TOWN BUS STATION

The town bus station was an active beating heart
With buses leaving to every part
Of North Wales and Cheshire West,
Company staff always doing their best.

There was little shelter as we queued in line,
But buses were frequent and on time.
It still stands at the northern end of the town,
But has become a shadow, even before lockdown.

Aside the station where passengers alighted in sun or cold,
Stood Hanmers café, a social venue for young and old,
A meeting place for friends, a farewell to departing feet,
Shops and offices still stand opposite on our old King Street.

A Barbers' shop stood close across the adjacent road,
Next to the bus company's crew tea-room abode.
A chap from my village rented a chair,
The floor always covered in black, white, and grey hair.

The chat in the 'salon' centred on the Sport of Kings,
Odds on who, or what, will win at that day's meetings.
I would call in after my school day ended close by,
A 'short back and sides', as men called in for things to buy.

The incessant chat on betting gossip and tips,
Was annoying my chap as he cut my hair with his 'clips'.
He asked me to run an errand to the nearby Post Office,
Send him a telegram, slipping me the text
and half a crown, for the service.

The telegram contained a tip from some 'racing stables',
Which I wrote and it was sent back to him to 'turn the tables.'
I mention this for many tips are unreliable or untrue,
So, know your friends or come the day that you will rue.

In those days, our buses provided a social setting,
A sit down after hours of shopping,
A chat, a laugh, a friendship made.
Then came cars, shopping malls, the Amazon brigade.

MY INCOME TAX – Now and Later!

An HMR&C Summary sheet to me was sent
To tell me how my tax was spent.
A helpful Table and a coloured chart,
It really is a work of art.

The facts are clear to some extent,
A near quarter on 'Welfare' was spent,
A fifth has gone to Health, that's good,
And six percent keeps me safe from 'Hoods'.
A similar amount defends us all from ills
And double was spent developing mind and skill.

One percent for each of four departments was spent
On street lighting, aid abroad, culture, and the environment.
Two percent to run the scheme, I don't begrudge it,
And a smidgeon went to the European budget.

I pay my dues from my pension plate,
My hard-earned pension and that from the State,
Behold! Fourteen percent goes back
to the State pension account!
And half again, interest on our National Debt amount!

With COVID-19 pandemic that last item will surely alter,
Depending upon how much our output did falter.
With temporary closures and workers on furlough,
Can we recover, maintain our jobs, and spend our dough.

The circle of employment and trade may have been weakened.
What we earn governs how we live and what we spend.
Selling our goods in a world post-infection is now a new task,
But will our world be the same I have to ask?

Not so, we're now going green the PM decrees,
We have chopped down far too many trees.
We've poisoned the earth, the air, the sea,
What will it mean for you and me?

Two-stroke, four-stroke, and diesel cars
Will all be turned into metal bars.
39 million UK vehicles will meet their fate
What's the cost for you, me, and the State?

Gas boilers are now in the same fateful state,
We urgently need to rescue our earth's climate.
Be prepared to experience some financial pain,
Our future Tax demands with cause great strain.

BIG BROTHER 1954; BIG BROTHER 2020

The early era of live black and white TV dramas
May be remembered for a couple of sagas.
The Quartermass Experiment and 'Nineteen Eighty-Four',
George Orwell's novel adapted and screened in 'Fifty-Four.

Big Brother, a symbolic leader in a bureaucratic world,
Just a face for the government of Oceania,
all-encompassing and bold,
To be adored and obeyed with futuristic purgatory,
Demoralising the family institution, prompting controversy.

Complaints of subversion and horror content,
Questions raised in Parliament and public discontent.
Controlling freedom of thought, with many
an horrendous scene,
Torture by rats, but was Orwell's foresight so obscene?

In recent years, dictatorial governments we can all see,
Bureaucrats, sufferings, internal conflicts due to tribal loyalty.
No freedom of thought, of speech, of independent living,
Big Brother, a fictional novel has turned into the real thing.

Today, Orwell's tale of futuristic purgatory
Is no longer of the future nor a fictional story.
Big Brother has moved into everyone's home and life,
The internet's global network is creating family strife.

Its adored and obeyed; it's constant, instant, and addictive,
A global network that is coercive and seductive.
Outweighing any benefits as it controls our daily living,
Affecting and distorting young minds so unforgiving.

Fantasy to reality, from the 'Fifties to the new 'Twenties,
From a rogue government's face to endless faceless entities.
'No reply' correspondence, scams, and unsuitable content,
Orwell's premise for 1984 was written with good intent.

His forecast was of a time of constant propaganda TV,
One channel and surveillance by a camera as you sit
upon your settee.
The slogan at the time offered the vision
"Big Brother is watching you watching television".

We are watching TV for more hours than we sleep,
Addicted to an internet site so worryingly deep.
Are we losing our breadth of life and living?
Seduced by todays Big Brother technology all consuming.

OUR GARDEN THIS NIGHT

The winter moon so full, so round, so bright,
Lighting up our garden here tonight.
The stillness of a frozen land all around,
Ethereal, a wonderland with no sound.

Our new Jubilee rose in still composure,
Winter jasmine droops down, its flowers in closure.
A white frozen sheen lies over the lawn,
I am witnessing the start of another cold dawn.

The land is held in a petrified hush,
The leafless skeleton of our tall smoke bush.
Only a month or so was in a flaming flush,
Stands strong with its bare branches all a flourish.

Another new year about to start,
Leaving a year that broke many a heart.
Kept families and friends so far apart,
And nursing care right off the chart.

The year began with a mystery,
A rotten old root from a long past tree,
Lying by a scraped out dusty cavity
And a damaged lawn for all to see.

Sunken pits all lie in the dry, dusty, ground
And patches of scraped out turf lying around.
This old codger blamed the birds for this,
Seeking dust baths and food, but he was amiss.

Birds do not pull over a large pot of carrots,
They prefer seeds, worms, and juicy maggots.
This old codger thought that's enough
And bought a night camera, all modern stuff.

A trail camera set out to film
Any visitor true and good.
Revealed a lone badger, so slim,
Clearly seeking around for food.

This lonely badger had come to see
What he could choose for his late-night tea.
For this old codger now the culprit he could see
Who dug up the root of an old boundary tree.

Surprise, surprise, the garden vandal was revealed,
The evidence was there, its future now was sealed,
And this old codger lowered his head in shame,
The garden birds had taken all the blame.

A lonesome animal, no friends nor family, on the loose,
Homeless and hungry, perhaps it will accept a truce.
Called the local badger group for some advice,
It's protected by law, but not my garden, well that's nice!

Only way to stop it entering the premises is clear,
Block every gap and hole, but can it climb an overhung tree
Or dig down low almost to a seam of coal?
I could spray the boundary with potions of old.

Had a chat with the suffering folks next door,
United effort to ban this omnivorous bore.
Blocked his entry at every point and location,
Sent him off to find another potential food allocation.

But this old codger may well become forlorn,
The animal now knows where food is grown.
Strong in limb and with excavating skill too,
Just have to stay up late and shout out "Shoo".

It came time and time again from next door,
It found the carrots before I could store.
Searching here and there, scratching for grubs.
It arrives just after closing of our local pubs.

It disappeared, left us in peace,
Must have found a better feast.
I wonder how this lonesome beast
Is coping with this winter from the east?

Our badger's a symbol of the life of many,
Lonely, homeless, lost, and hungry.
This same winter moon shines on us all,
Some stand tall, whilst others have hit the wall.

The badger is a protected animal, that's swell,
But vulnerable humans need full protection as well.

P.S. HE'S BACK!

He's back! our black and white omnivorous mammal,
Attacked my tulip beds of bulbs, yes, it's my badger pal.
All was fine last time I looked around,
Today, carnage and he has now gone to ground.

How did he enter my garden, I ask?
No sign of gap or under-fence digging task.
Wherever he's been since last time he called,
His dinners there have clearly stalled.

It was the Spring nights of Twenty-Twenty,
When this dear lad came with stomach empty.
Nightly visits and some desecration of lawn and plants,
Enjoying Michelin star cuisine despite my rants.

Tonight, the camera will be set up again
To film this guy and information gain.
There are more tulip beds he has not found,
He will search and find them, I'll be bound.

The videos show no trace, just a cat or two,
Filming the tulips left untouched all night through.
I'll try again tonight to check and see
If our friend visited just with thoughts nostalgically.

He's reappeared just once, at the end of Lent,
Living within this concrete urban environment.
A lonesome ranger strong and bold,
Yes! this badger has survived the winter cold.

pps He came back for the rest of our tulips!!

WORKING FROM HOME

'Working from home' is the new office dimension,
'Working at home' is to avoid any office tension,
'Working in the home' is a job with no pension,
Working at all is the new level of apprehension.

Attics have been cleared of forgotten gear,
That's hung around up there for many a year.
Flooring laid and stud walls constructed,
Ladders dropped down and wiring extended.

Garages emptied, no longer take the car,
Desk and chair installed, internet to talk near and far.
Zooming reveals many telling background scenes,
Distracting viewers with their 'office' décor themes.

Garden offices for those who can pay,
Or Dad's shed has had to make way,
Wrapped in blankets and finger mitts too,
It's fingers, not language, that turning blue.

That morning and evening traffic nightmare,
A thing of the past commuters had to share.
No need for tie and shirt, blouse, and skirt,
Set the alarm, you can't be late for the office date.

Just slip out of bed and toast some bread,
They will only see the top of your head,
Don't worry what's lying down below,
Stand up, and promotion you'll never know.

Know the code of Conference Zooming,
Meetings on-line are really booming.
To speak, raise your hand up like a post,
But beware, not with it full of toast.

Do not lean in and get too close
To show the hairs growing in your nose.
One would never stand so near,
Except that office guy who likes to leer.

Do not reveal your mug of coffee,
Or latest gin for all to see,
The dog or cat sitting on your knee,
It's Zooming etiquette you see.

Office life is a thing of the past,
No corridor chats, no gossip cast.
A devious stroll, empty file in hand,
No gathering together of your lunchtime band.

Your office block now stands empty and alone,
With other shops and stores all forlorn.
Amazon will rent the building stock,
I guess we're all in for a commercial shock.

LIFE IN THE 1970's

And Prompted Thoughts

Bloody Sunday, unions unrest across the nation,
Petrol shortages, the dead unburied situation.
Highest inflation, IMF loan of several billion,
North Sea oil, and 16 Concordes costing £650 million.

The 1970's, a turbulent period by general consent,
Like Labour, the Sex Pistols and Punk came and went,
Mrs Thatcher, Iron Lady, then grabbed the union bone.
And the Wurzels rose to number one!

During that era, I undertook a period of research study,
Visual Perception, spatial perception, and acuity.
How our eyes and brain work, and rods and cones,
Allow me, briefly, to 'pick the meat from the bones'.

When light passes in through the eye's lens
Onto the retina wall of rods and cone cells, it bends.
An upside-down image is transferred by electric energy
To the brain which turns our world the way we see.

As I sit here pondering what will be,
How and what do animals see?
550 million years ago, distance back not infinitesimal
When eyes were first formed in an emerging animal.

Dogs' eyes capture and process yellows and blues
But not the rainbow's range of colourful hues
Like those humans who are colour blind
They cannot see red which is a bind.

Cows have long eyelashes to filter dust,
Young ladies, I'm sure, for such will lust.
Their pupils, not round, oval shaped instead,
Can see in the dark, but they can't see red.

Goats have exceptional eyesight around the clock,
Unique in the world of farming stock.
See almost around themselves for anything evil,
No tear ducts but horizontal slits for each eye pupil.

Parallel to the ground with panoramic views,
Good for grazing and guarding lambs and ewes.
From grey shades they can recognise yellow and blue,
Orange and violet and green too.

With horizontal slit pupils they see better at night,
Not blinded by headlamps or our daytime sunlight.
They are not colour blind in any way, nor supercilious,
Just sociable, independent, and very curious.

WHEN TWO BECAME THREE

No Fathers Allowed

Snow lay deep that special New Year,
It ended the previous Christmas cheer.
Cause for concern for my wife and I, you see
Our family of two was about to become three.

Frozen traffic ruts in the deep soiled snow
Were now paths to walk, but very slow,
Icicles of stalactite form hung from the gutter,
Steaming breath if any word you utter.

From home to Maternity was just one street,
RAF Hospital, single storey, but quite neat.
The signs were there, we have to go
Along the ruts in the deep slippery snow.

On the ward a bed was chosen,
"You can go now!", an order quite frozen,
"Ring tomorrow" and shown the door,
Dads not welcome, that's for sure.

Sat alone, such peace will not last
When junior arrives and starts to blast.
Will it be a boy or girl to arrive?
Rather, will it be delivered safely alive.

The snow still lies deep the very next day,
Find a phone and coins to pay.
Apprehension, as the number is dialled
Click, into the phone the coins are piled.

"No change" the lady said emphatically,
"Visiting time for fathers is at three."
My wife is waiting for me when I visit,
Patience needed as we just talk and sit.

The birth is clearly going to be slow,
The baby knows there's too much snow,
It's nice and warm inside of mummy,
And there's no stretch marks on her tummy.

Day one passes and through the night,
Phoned next morning at first daylight.
"Visiting for fathers is at three."
I hope I can have a cup of tea.

Day two passes and through the night,
Phoned next morning at first daylight.
"Congratulations! It's a girl; see her at three."
Telegrams sent; they will be met with glee.

The Churching of Women followed the event,
A common service with good intent.
Thanksgiving for safe deliverance, new life on earth,
Preservation from problems of giving childbirth.

Post-natal care will last for some time,
Care for junior and mum back to her prime.
Time to warm the little one's den,
No central heating or double glazing then.

Off to buy a small electric heater,
Must not let the cold wind enter.
A thermometer is hung on the new Den wall,
'Maintain the temperature' is the call.

The baby 'bible' was by Dr Spock,
He knew that child-care can be a shock.
Six foot four, he loved and lived on the sea,
Fifty million sought his book and so did we.

The snow has melted; it's Spring, we're glad,
And spring is in the step of Mum and Dad,
As baby's conveyed in her coach sprung pram
By proud parents with their new-born lamb.

WHEN THREE BECAME FOUR

No Fathers Allowed!

Two years later, same time, same place,
Cold dry weather, no sign of ice.
Our daughter was soon to have a pal,
Would it be a boy, or would it be a gal?

The first delivery was long in coming,
Minor surgery solved the waiting.
Anxious parents hope for an easier time,
Bag is packed, so just waiting for a sign.

Our two-year-old is tucked up in bed so tight,
A neighbour agrees to sit, so that's alright.
Mill Lane, a larger house than last time is home,
Thankfully, is even closer to the delivery room.

Our Ford Thames van, bought to hold the pram,
Takes Mum the short run, must keep her warm.
Arrived and to the ward we walked and waited,
Mother examined, with breadths abated.

Expectation began to rise with some intent,
At nine o' clock, father to the TV lounge was sent.
The BBC news had just begun and so had the birth
Before the half-hour news ended there was great mirth.

A daughter has arrived safe and sound, and full of life,
Dad retrieved from the TV lounge to join his wife.
Relief all round, this birth will make so many happy,
And it also coincided with the birth of "Jackie".**

Mother and child rested on the ward for days,
Post-natal care for a length of time always pays.
Telegrams of joy, which then prompted aid,
No paternity leave, but second child allowance paid.

Mair came to support her working son and his daughter
When mum and baby went home, in-law Madge took over.
Spring arrived; post-natal checks were all 'on song',
All was well for this settled family, but not for long.

Dad receives notice of a posting south; that's the rule,
To Buckinghamshire's Chiltern hillside military school.
Moving on with a family so young is quite a task,
Planning, packing, cleaning, was a big ask.

A great deal of work fell on mother's shoulders now,
But multiskilled and organised, she did not bow.
The family moved to the Rothchild's old estate
With training camp and large hospital there 'on a plate'.

Life was fine, two young cherubs with golden hair,
NAAFI stores, country air, and medical care.
But would this settled situation survive?
Or would four now become five.

** *A Magazine for Girls*

96

WHEN FOUR BECAME FIVE

No Fathers Allowed!

The year was 1966 and summer had arrived,
The family of four is expecting to become five.
Pop Culture is rife and, so too, the mini skirt,
The Monkeys "I'm a believer" the charts' top hit.

Neil Diamond has US success with 'Cherry, Cherry',
World Boxing Champion is Mohammad Ali.
And we all know of our only World Cup win
When England beat Germany, there was a hell of a din.

The new Severn Bridge let the English in on the M4
A very long way round was the route before.
This family and country all in excited mode and gay,
But things took a turn on August Bank Holiday Monday.

Concerns were raised over the health of babe and mum,
Month of hospital care took mum away from home.
Mair came to give Dad and girls some sustenance,
As mum was away under constant surveillance.

Visiting times allowed only adults to visit,
Mum apart from her little ones, an awful split.
Midnight arrived on September the fourth
And shortly after another bundle of joy came forth.

As dawn broke, telephone box call broke the news
A sister for the girls, a red head through and through.
The waiting sisters each received a gift,
A pram like mum's, to give them a lift.

Dad went to the Mess that night and joined a pal,
Once again, to celebrate the birth of this little gal.
Met the consultant who delivered number three
"Hoped for a boy?" he asked.
'No, just a healthy honeybee.'

The long post-natal care stay needed a tweak,
Mother and cherub wanted home in a week.
And the red headed lass let it be known,
The staff were glad when she went home.

This new-born babe was keen to be seen
And heard; never before has there been
Such a commotion for many a night,
Challenging the staff, this little mite.

No-one could sleep, no one could speak,
The noise could be heard down in the street.
From the new-borns to Matron, enough was enough,
Off to a sound-proof place with comfort and warmth.

This bundle of fun went home with mum,
A family of five is now the sum.
All settled and growing and having fun.
A posting! We're off again to live in the sun.

WHEN FIVE BECAME SIX

No Fathers Allowed!

Like Enid Blyton's "Five go off to the seaside"
The family packed up, said goodbye, no one cried.
Malta is the destination for this family group,
Flown by members of the RAF Transport troupe.

The island still in recovery mode from war and hell
Was untouched by tourists, not one high-rise hotel.
Bands led festival parades through narrow streets,
Church bells ringing, home-made fireworks,
and cheesy treats.

A different life, change of pace and very strong heat,
New landscape vision, Mediterranean Sea, hot car seat!
Two older girls went to RAF schools by bus,
One little cherub to nursery by mini car and never a fuss.

As time went by and island politics were under strain,
Tourism, the call to bolster the island's financial pain.
Air Malta was formed, hostesses sent to the UK to train,
The people voted and broke the old political chain.

British forces' role and presence was not required,
Libyan support for the island was about to be hired.
The tour of duty for the family of five came to an end
Just before all the British troops left the
George Cross island.

This family of five had enjoyed their time
on this war-torn isle,
Friends they made, local people they met
that made them smile.
They left as they came but not quite the same,
For the five was soon to up their game!!

Back to Blighty and Lincolnshire's flat land.
RAF College Cranwell with no sea or sand.
No neighbouring military hospital to make life easy
Should anyone get sick or feel quite queasy.

The nearest military maternity unit at Nocton Hall
Was some fifteen miles through country lanes.
Mair arrived to help, she answered the family call,
That time in June '71 when mum was having pains.

The usual ban on dads' attendance,
Morning call for latest delivery stance,
It's a boy! and both are doing their best,
Visiting for Dads only, after lunchtime rest.

A healthy boy to keep up the family surname,
His sisters excited, what will now be his name?
All in the car, so travelled safe and slow,
Girls see their new brother, from the ward's window.

Post-natal care complete and now back home,
This little bundle will soon be ready to roam
Around the home, garden, and Brauncewell Road,
And he always did as he was told.

Enjoying constant attendance from his sisters
They were so delighted with his presence.
He had his own version of CBBC
As they danced around him full of glee.

His arrival at Cranwell was in good company,
Prince Charles had joined the first Graduate Entry
To learn how to fly military style,
Whilst this little babe was learning how to smile.

Top of the Pops on that day, in the sign of Cancer?
"Chirpy, Chirpy, Cheep, Cheep" is the answer.

He and his sisters have made their marks
With their partners creating ten more sparks
To lighten the world with knowledge and skill
Bringing happiness to the two who started together,
before the pill!

MY WAR-TIME CUISINE

As the enemy tried to starve our nation,
Attacking food conveys in the Atlantic Ocean.
Imported food and fruit were in short supply,
Rationing and 'Dig for Britain' was the cry.

Home grown potatoes, fruit, and local fish,
A housewife's challenge to create a dish.
The 'national loaf' of wholemeal bread,
Aided one's meal, it has to be said.

When time prevailed for my village miners,
They dug their gardens, won 'Rose Show' prizes.
My own back garden had been set to please,
With pre-war planting of fruit bushes and trees.

But family gardeners had been killed or married a lass,
The trees and bushes now choked by grass.
When mother and I moved in to provide nursing care,
My father at war unable to share.

Despite the grass and little care,
Gooseberries, apples, and a Conference pear
Provided fresh vitamins during the war-time struggle,
Hens and a couple of roosters in our garden jungle.

To augment our rations bought at our registered shop,
Mother replaced those older hens given the chop
And plucked and cooked to help meet our table need,
With baby chicks, the cycle then to proceed.

Free range in every way, one knocking on our door,
Seeking the comfort of our nearby bathroom floor!
The uncut grass growing around the gooseberry bushes
Was a perfect nest to lay one's eggs, like swans in rushes.

Nothing ever wasted, boiled potato peelings mash
Mixed with feed, a chicken's delicious hash.
A young chap living nearby provided rabbits deceased,
Mother then skinned and the lead shot released!

Folk talked of chocolate, bananas, and other delights,
Children's books provided those black and white sights.
For collecting paper to aid the war effort in school,
Canada sent powdered chocolate which I greedily
ate like a fool.

School morning milk and lunchtime meals
Ensured we all enjoyed good healthy deals
For nursery children awaiting formal schooling
Orange juice with cod liver oil kept them even keeling.

War ended but rationing went on into the 'Fifties.
Recovery a challenge, but cuisine was slowly eased
And fed me until I reached my early 'teens.
Behold! a healthy diet it now seems.

This brief review requires a background context,
Nightly blackouts with fear of what is coming next
As 'Gerry' flew overhead to deliver carnage,
What will be the headline on tomorrow's front page?

Not knowing when this war will end,
Will friendly nations muster troops and send
To stand shoulder to shoulder, man to man,
Or will we receive that dreaded telegram?

LOCK DOWN IN THE GARDEN

My garden shrubs went into lockdown,
As Autumn days turned the green leaves brown.
Isolated, plant by plant, in stark repose,
Awaiting spring Growmore and the garden hose.

My wife and I have endured a lockdown too,
Our hair did not turn brown, it just grew and grew.
No-one to meet, remote, isolated, alone,
Restless, frustrated, like chewing a bone.

Time will come when buds emerge too soon,
Just to be nipped by frost on a night of full moon.
A clever person will cover all with fleece,
A true member of the garden police.

Fools have emerged from lockdown state,
To dance and play and drink, the law they hate.
Our Chief has made many a plea,
Stay home, stay safe, and just drink tea.

The lawn was given its Autumn feed,
But rain spread down at quite a speed.
What will remain when Spring days arrive?
Areas of grass may have taken a watery dive.

The virus spread around with a similar rate,
We were too late to shut the gate.
What will be the loss of life and employment?
Reminding all that nothing on earth is permanent.

We have enjoyed our regular supermarket drop
But will any of our Malls still have an open shop?
Gardens will need an expensive renovation
And, truly, a far more costly one for our nation.

The natural world will awake and blossom
Trees and shrubs burst forth from top to bottom
Will we watch this happen from our windowpane?
Or walking hand in hand down a country lane.

So, dig for Britain as we did in the war,
Pull up your sleeves, don't pull a 'jar'.
Clear out the weeds, the waste, the idle,
Cut out bureaucracy and those on the fiddle.

The efforts put in on any Spring day,
With spade and fork on sand or clay.
When we are released, so tentatively,
Our Summer days should be quite heavenly.

POST WAR VILLAGE LIFE

War is over, peace has eventually come to pass,
Men and women now safely back home, but alas
Memorials erected to recognise the fallen,
And broken hearts that will now need mending.

My mining village men had played their part,
Toiling day and night with all their heart
To keep the war machine running non-stop,
Now all brought together as one nationalised crop.

Recovery was slow, ration books, and shortages,
But village life was returning in progressive stages.
Flower show, carnival, and local sporting events,
Madam Gwen, and her juvenile performers 'presents'.

Pantomimes in the Miners Welfare Institution.
Cast of sixty budding thespians, their annual production.
The sprung dance floor protected with cocoa mat flooring,
Fold flat chairs for temporary seating.

Rehearsals weekly during the Autumn Quarter,
Help was sought from my mother, a local dressmaker,
Now wardrobe mistress, mammoth task in a limited time
Providing several costumes for principals and chorus line.

She attended rehearsals for measuring and fitting,
Took me along. I watched from where I was sitting.
'Why don't you join us?' said Madam Gwen,
'You can do a number, as and when'

Partnered up with a pretty girl called Megan,
A continuity role was the running script plan.
Front of curtain as scenes had to change,
We sang our hearts out, with limited range.

Each with actions and movement to suit,
The band in full support to boot.
'I've got a lovely bunch of coconuts' was one,
'Feeding the ducks on the pond', another song.

With sixty cast and several changes of costume,
For weeks filling our council house front room.
Dresses in all colours, shapes, and sizes, hanging there,
Costumes, hats, cotton reels; pins and needles beware.

A large cast of youngsters and leading seniors,
Full nightly audiences with sore posteriors!
All enjoying an evening of family fun,
Simple pleasures to repair the wartime glum.

I'LL GET BACK TO YOU

"I'll get back to you"
This 'get out' clause is not new,
All too often this promise is not met,
It's guaranteed to frustrate and upset.

You wait and wait in anticipation,
A dissolving mood of expectation.
Did they call when I was in the garden?
Too late now, should they seek a pardon.

A written promise is even worse,
Permanently on display makes one curse.
Should I ring and speak to someone,
Ah! all I get is their ringing tone.

This old codger has witnessed this effect,
Tradesmen guilty of customer neglect,
Public services' staff under stress,
Over worked, under pressure, in a mess.

This old codger was engaged for many years
Reviewing unresolved complaints and subsequent tears,
Across the NHS and Social Services in Wales,
Many developed when this response fails.

Do not generate problems for yourselves,
With clients' feelings of being left on their shelves.
Do not make promises you fail to deliver,
Their trust and support you will never recover.

OUR PRESENT WORLD

I had hoped to reach a time in my life,
Sit back, relax with my dear old wife,
But our world is in such a state of strife,
Demonstrations, riots, and discontent so rife.

Violence is now too frequent on our streets,
iPhones to record and constant TV news repeats.
Racial abuse, female abuse, bullying, and rape,
Tormentors transmitting behind their i.t. cape.

Drugs are prevalent, a modern form of currency
For those pushing many addictive lives into misery.
Knives and blades have replaced the pocket kerchief,
Far more violent than the old petty thief.

Peaceful marches to express concerns, seeking change,
Highjacked by thugs, intent on mindless damaging carnage,
Emerging at night like wild animals let out of their cage.
Hooded, masked, egged on into a rage.

Is it the web, with no active control of decency?
Detached from community life, just constant indoor TV?
Family lives in crisis, unable to maintain their role or duty?
Teenage years schooling in an obstreperous academy?

It's just a few that tarnish the name of respect and love,
It was just 'The Few' that lost their lives in the skies above
So we may live in peace and cast off all violence and furore.
Honour our sisters and brothers with their faiths,
many now living in terror.

Change is on-going, failure to accept it would be an error,
Respect, decency, order, responsibility, we cannot surrender.

Those worldwide in high office with duty to set an example,
Their behaviour, greed, truthfulness, each a sample
Of what we see, as we struggle to manage our daily life.
Who will stop our world declining into turmoil and strife?

It's you and me, citizens of a world that's in distress,
With compassion and tolerance, let's reduce the stress.
Recognise each other's faiths and cultures,
And historical adherence by their fathers and mothers.

John Lennon asked us to 'imagine' in his song,
'That the world will live as one' and get along.
A blending of nations with their unique variety,
So let us sing together with voices in harmony.

A symphony of acknowledged sympathy,
An anthem of solidarity,
A hymn of international democracy,
A chorale of world-wide unity.

Parenting

First you give them roots,
Then you give them wings.

Dr Jonas Salk, Physician.

ANIMAL SENTIENCE AND ANIMAL RIGHTS

I have just enjoyed a meal of venison,
With a glass of red wine, together in unison.
Was the beast bred for the table?
Or culled; to enjoy life, sadly, it was no longer able.

Turkeys are bred for the Christmas season,
Fed and watered for no other reason.
Chickens galore are created all around the world,
Mass produced, automatic feeding, then sold.

Some animals and birds are raised to feed those nations
Where many people are living on water and basic rations.
The life span of these creatures is often no greater
Than the period of time required by the customer's order.

This way of farming stretches far back in life,
From a beast traded in for a future wife,
To settle a dispute, or a period of armed strife,
Now cultivated at speed to sustain our human life.

We moved from finding food to hunting food,
From hunting food to corralling the best and good.

Animal welfare, animal sentience
These are questions for our conscience
Do they have feelings and emotions like me?
Experience joy and pleasure? Are they pain free?

Are we violating animal rights?
Can some rights reflect our human rights?
They have rights of care and protection,
Health, and shelter from ills and infection.

Human rights in the Declaration are far reaching,
Ignored by some nations, despite the preaching.
The Declaration is an international law to uphold
Of life and liberty, the requirements are so bold.

There is one freedom that can also apply to both,
Free from slavery and torture, action I loathe.
This treatment to animals and humans is a sin,
A crime so evil, carried out by man
just raises my adrenalin.

OLD NAIN JONES

Old Nain Jones sits by her front room window,
Her lace net curtains hanging still and low,
Watching life on the street outside,
With memories of when it was cleaned with pride.

Old Ted is out there still delivering coal,
Once a fine young man, played in goal.
Ah! Young Nell has just caught his eye,
As she struts her stuff passing by.

Tom 'pony', with his dicky bow so new,
Chatting to the neighbours as councillors do.
He'll not get Nain's vote any more,
Even if he comes knocking on her door.

Reverend Aurelius walks by in earnest,
His long black cassock not at its best,
Safety pinned, he's christened, married, buried many,
Rarely carries money, not even a penny.

He lives by candlelight, as so many others do,
Times home visits when he senses a pot of stew.
His old purple clerical bag provides some daily ease,
A bible, bread, and a lump of cheese.

There's 'Flowing Health' now passing by so slowly,
Bent over by years of toil and worry,
Off to buy her daily paper from Dai Thomas' shop,
And her usual bottle of Penderyn 'pop'.

114

A slight shift of the well-worn curtain net,
To catch 'Fat Jack' off to place his bet.
Stops to chat to that floozy Nell,
His wife will surely give him hell.

'Midnight Gwen' just left on the afternoon town bus,
Nain Jones knows well what goes on in that metropolis.
"Brazen lass" she utters, her closing curtain in need of repair,
Sitting back in her antimacassar covered armchair.

Old Nain Jones sits daily by her front room window,
Those memories were of times when things were slow,
Now tarnished by the life she sees,
A life where no one ever says thanks or please.

A life of instant gratification,
Spreading throughout our divided nation.
No Sunday chapel in modest dress and hat,
Bodies now revealing coloured ink of this and that.

Old Nain Jones is a lonely soul I fear,
Has lost her friends and loved ones dear.
Overtaken by a life so changed, so fast,
Seeks comfort from the memories of her past.

We old codgers do our best to keep on top,
But on occasions we mutter 'it has to stop'.
But as change continues, it's direction that matters,
Get it wrong, and the world will end up in tatters.

SCRAP YARDS GALORE

In a desert place with dry flat sand,
Redundant aircraft in a line they stand,
Outdated, inefficient, too big, too small,
Superfluous to the industry's current call.

I fear that there will be many, many, more
Surplus to airline fleets, left on the floor,
Whilst this virus occupies our air and more,
The world not vaccinated until 'Twenty-Four'.

On a concrete runway of an old airfield,
Stands rows of new cars ever waiting a deal.
Your new car may not be as new as you think,
The motor industry must be on the brink.

What to do with your diesel car or van,
Very soon such vehicles will suffer a ban.
Petrol too is for the chop as well,
It's electric soon, but will they sell?

Millions of cars with polluting fuel,
Hordes of technicians each with a dismantling tool,
Shredding the leather, plastic, rubber parts,
Breaking many owners' bank accounts and hearts.

The cost of change to this transportation asset,
Grown like Topsy with no regard and no respect.
Cut down to size on world health grounds,
Pollution, infection, and financial worrying sounds.

We shall all have to take stock and tighten our belts,
Cut out luxuries even down to those chocolate melts.
Cut our cloth lest we wear just rags,
No more sangria nor duty free fags.

OUR COVID-19 JAB

The telephone rang, "Hello" I said pensively,
Was this another caller trying to scam me?
Computer-generated calls, bane of my life,
"Calling to arrange jabs for you and your wife".

At last, our names have now been reached,
The order of jabbing has not been breached,
"Tomorrow, five past two, at your surgery",
I hope the process is not purgatory.

A short queue outside the block,
The cold air may nullify any post-jab shock,
As several nurses were wielding their syringe,
For faint-hearted old codgers some may cringe.

The needle glinted in the afternoon sun
But I was seated and not ready to run.
An armful of AstraZeneca for my future safeguard
And my personal COVID-19 record card.

We waited our post-op time nearby,
Patiently we sat, my wife and I,
Just the same as far as we could see,
So homeward bound for a cup of tea.

When my wife and I had checked in,
A lady escort took us under her wing.
Asked if she had just come back from lunch,
"No time. Just grabbed a bite!". What a bunch
Of selfless angels serving across our countryside,
They should all hold their heads up high with pride.

This glorious army of men and women
At the sharp end, not pushing a pen
Quietly, they tend and care for us
Dealing with each challenge without a fuss.

They are not angels in the sky,
They walk and run, they do not fly,
They care, they nurse, sometimes they sigh,
You'll never know them as you walk by.

WALES: LAND OF SONG

Wales has been the land of song,
In church, in chapel, or touchline throng,
Soft clear tenors, deep rich bass,
In competitions, we always set the pace.

A desire to sing in harmony,
In Welsh, or English, in any key,
To entertain, to raise much needed money,
Choir practice twice weekly, all for charity.

Each mining village was well endowed
With choral voices all good and sound.
Men who toiled in the bowels of our land,
Stood shoulder to shoulder, proud and grand.

Enduring many episodes of danger and fear,
Human resilience tested, in that foul atmosphere,
Reflected in their emotional singing,
Heart rendering voices all a' blending.

Mines have closed, bonds are broken,
Unity, friendships split asunder.
That common thread with no word spoken
Singing together was a choral wonder.

'Comrades in Arms' will never sound the same,
For old mining comrades have left the stage.
For me, current unison pieces are rather tame
I've witnessed the closure of a magical, musical page.

WALKING DOWN THE OLD TOWN STREETS

Wander down the old town streets,
With shopping bags and a twist of sweets.
Passing by familiar faces, familiar shops,
Ah! there's a window full of juicy chops.

Mingling along with many earnest shoppers
As they pop in and out to spend their coppers,
A chat or two to catch up with the news
Or gossip, and the current state of the old town's loos.

Butchers, bakers, coffee makers,
Chemists, newsagents selling daily papers.
Fishmongers, iron monger, saddler too,
Gents' outfitters, haberdashers, boot, and shoe.

Barbers, salons, bookshops, grocers, provisions and green,
Tea shops to rest those aching toes, no longer sweet sixteen.
Health shops, florists, wine merchants, and pubs,
Marks & Spencer, Woolworths, those enormous hubs.

Into the butchers with its sawdust floor
To buy from a smiling obliging fellow,
A piece of beef and a meaty 'dog' bone,
Two good meals for the price of one.

Indoor markets, and market traders out on the shout,
Fruit and veg, rolls of materials too many to count.
Carpets, rugs, the odd herb and plant,
Not an ounce of plastic to supplant.

Back home the village shops are run by villagers,
Not on Sundays, it's a day of rest for all retailers.
Our village Co-op stands on stilts – a wooden store,
With its recognised scent of cheese, bacon and more.

A small office to collect each daily milk token,
An open tin of mixed biscuits, stands alone,
some sadly broken.
The staff's fixed positions behind a horseshoe of counters,
Machine slices smoothly through a ham joint as it enters.

Leading the field with their 'divi' promotion,
A company for the people, a sound invention.
My Saturday job, grandmother's weekly order,
Come back with a dented tin and I was in a bother!

Alas, one stop shopping, supermarket stadiums now rife,
Changing the retail scene and our way of life.
Muzak drowns out any chance of casual chat,
Like those town shop keepers with a jaunty hat.

Just slide your goods across a screen,
Obey instructions or wait to be seen.
'Place item in your bag', 'Pass item through again',
Then wave your card to pay for the pain.

Like the Indian summers in late September,
Those early retail days that I remember
Met the needs of our local population,
Now, we are facing a human explosion.

How to meet the world's food demand?
'Five loaves and two fishes' are beyond this land.
Alas, cheap food to meet the First World's greed
And satisfy the Third World's need.

COVID-19: A SELF ASSESSMENT

Lockdown, or incarceration, has worn me down,
I'm crashing around like a demented clown.
Who, how, what, caused this world epidemic?
Millions dead and more millions sick.

These long winter nights, confined after tea,
Same old faces on my colour TV
Trying to resurrect game shows of old,
Destined to fail, they should have been told.

Our medical cupboard is full to the brim,
With potions for her and tubes for him.
Cream for spots, lumps, and tools to trim,
But really, they all should be put in the bin.

Our bottle box is out with the bin,
It's full to the top displaying our sin.
To any publican, it is a delight to see,
Dogs come a'sniffing, I hope they don't pee!

My car has been called for a service and MOT,
We have not been in it, our family to see.
I've forgotten the routes, so I'll use my Sat-Nav.
Hell! I've forgotten how, I really have.

With mask and sanitiser, I handed the key.
The showroom so empty, a sad sight to see.
No cars adorned with prices and additional 'treats',
In one door, follow the arrows, and out to the street.

I've forgotten how to walk, or how to talk,
But I have not forgotten how to measure time.
At the Post Office, "First or Second" she squawked,
Damn it! I started to reply in rhyme.

When this is all over, if ever it be,
Call up the Heads of every country,
To account for their actions and inactions too.
How, when did this begin and allowed to spread like goo.

I've lived through an era of wonderful international events,
Not scarred, as our fathers found it their fate
and no way to prevent.
I fear we've created a world so uncaring, so unchecked,
My children's children will now need to address and correct.

Tackle ignorance, greed, and avarice in every way,
Open wide the eyes of those with no horizons, no aid, no stay.
Educate the world of right and wrong, let them have a say,
An obligation, a contribution, a part to play.

Whilst robots take over supply of the essentials of life,
Use your creativity to tackle world peace and strife.
Ease pain and suffering, prevent starvation and thirst,
Spread love and understanding 'till all hearts just burst.

OUR ZOOM ANNIVERSARY

It's our family zooming anniversary day,
A year of face-to-face chat and have our say.
We all sign-in to our email call,
Sundays' weekly update on the health of all.

Mute button is off or is it on?
Frozen image, a signal somewhere going wrong,
Hair styles reflecting salons closed and bare,
Home-made cakes revealed but no family to share.

The state of the pandemic discussed in earnest,
The conflicting liberties allowed in the east or west.
When will we be able to meet and hug?
What is the current state of this invisible bug?

"I have had my jab" one member announces,
"Should have shed a few pounds and ounces
Or worn a sleeveless top for ease,
The nurse assisted, happy to please."

"I'm still waiting" another declared,
"Mum and I will have ours paired".
The chat moves on to face mask wearing,
No one can hear you talking or swearing!

Our weekly zoom gathering comes to an end,
Thanks to technology, our love we send.
For 52 weeks, 72 hours, we have met together,
So near, yet so far, in a digital tether.

We'll meet again next week, same time, same place,
No end in sight whilst we all fail to keep our space.
We'll not talk parties, holidays, theatres, or festivals
Whilst we are restricted to life within our four walls.

We will just keep zooming every week,
Until this enemy has grown so weak
That folks can meet, and children play
And we know the cost and what we must pay.

The tragedy of lost world lives will be overwhelming,
The cost in jobs quite staggering.
Lessons to learn, organisational systems to replace,
But will it ever be a better place?

STOP THE WORLD, I WANT TO GET OFF

An Apology

An utterance of despair I would not scoff,
"Stop the world, I want to get off",
Littlechap pleaded, living his selfish life,
In the 1961 Newley-Bricusse story of human strife.

Searching for something better, always dissatisfied,
The grass is greener on the other side,
That old codger, like many more may pose,
Finally realised that what he sought was under his nose.

Now, we need to stop the world, it's time to change
Our lifestyle, greed, discontent, across the range.
Disharmony, brutality, inhumanity, all must end,
A world-wide message I have to send.

So, let us stop the world and start again,
There is now far too much grief and pain,
Excessive drought, excessive rain,
Our eco-system is under strain.

Stop the world and let us assess the situation,
An audit of each country's contribution
Towards our global maladministration,
And then seek a corrective course of action.

Stop the world, let's think it through,
Spell out what each country has to do.
Eliminate waste, and plastic too,
Feed the hungry, put every foot into a shoe.

Stop the world, it's out of balance,
Everyone needs equal sustenance.
Share our drinking water, bread, and food,
Protection from searing sun and flood.

Stop the world we cannot breathe,
There is so much we can achieve
If only we all worked together,
Clean air, clear water, stable weather.

I make no apology for my deep concerns,
For I am one who has seen the patterns,
The warning signs, the evidence now so clear,
The inaction by those who rule and those governing by fear.

I stand guilty of 'asleep at my post' with my peers,
Of contributing to the earth's sickness over the years.
Ignorance of cause and effect by what we have done,
Of action and reaction, and now we have a hotter sun.

My concerns have been expressed before,
I feel responsible looking back over 80 years and more.
On behalf of my fellow chums, most of late repose,
Apologies, for a poisoned chalice not a red, red, rose.

MY FATHER

My father's grandfather was a religious miner,
Temperance lifestyle and Chapel hymn writer.
Must have impacted on Winston, the first born,
And as life was liberated, he was torn.

A member of Boys Brigade and for what it stood,
He had a strong influence on doing good.
I guess no joy was ever present nor at the forefront
As WW1 took young lives at the Western Front.

My grandfather, too, was a miner often seeking work,
But my father's schooling he did not shirk.
Scholarship to the Town's Grammar School,
He was no dud, very keen, and no fool.

The family had a crisis, a mining fault,
And life had to come to an abrupt halt.
They moved away for family help and cover,
Father stayed for schooling living with his grandmother.

To help the family purse, my father did not shrink,
He left the Grammar school early, and pen and ink.
Gained the best paid job with the new transport omnibus,
He became a conductor, uniform, and with no fuss.

Later, he would become the guy sitting at the wheel,
Early drivers of public transport needed some steel.
Married my mother, a grand affair, a family show,
Dampened, her father lying in a mining grave below.

I came along in '37 as Europe's troubles were emerging,
War in '39, my father placed on the War Reserve listing,
At 31, called up in November '40 to RAF Padgate,
Morse Code and military duties brought him 'up to date'.

Posted to Burma, Signals Depot No 4 on a Naga Hill.
In '43 his truck slipped down a hillside, quite a spill.
So, into Kohima hospital for four long weeks,
To re-set his ribs, I guess with just a few painful tweaks.

Later this hospital was over-run as it stood
By Japanese troops, killing all that were doing good.

He told of a visit by the village elders, so slight,
To tell of Japanese soldiers seeking their hill camp site.
And of the night someone was scraping along his tent!
Challenged, he fired and killed a pig with no serious intent.

Living that life full of tension and stress,
But for my father it became more, not less.
His younger brother Clifford lost at sea,
On HMS Kite protecting a convoy in the Baltic Sea.

Thoughts about his mother, father, and his family,
Must have chased around his mind constantly.
Far from home and no support to give,
Total stress, total sadness; how would you live?

He often wrote home and sent many a home-made card,
Heavily censored, on photographic paper quite hard.
His base was one of many along the hillside,
On the India/Burma front where the Japanese did hide.

Passing messages to HQ on data of flight movements,
Battles on every hill and valley, troops all living in tents.

The forgotten war came to a stop.
Troops shipped home slowly, not a hop.
My father met a guy on board his ship
Pushing Communism during the trip.

No doubt men were bitter, felt forgotten,
Considered life had turned out rotten
And wars should never occur again
With so many colleagues caught and slain.

A short time back home and it happened,
A parcel arrived which my mother opened,
Communist leaflets spilled out, quite 'hot',
My father was ordered to burn the lot.

Men return from war with all forms of stress,
From an all-male lifestyle, fixed times, and dress.
Struggling to readjust to unrestricted life,
Forgetting the growth of their babes and wife.

Eager to impress on returning home, with knowledge,
Changed the single switch lighting in our 'through room'
To two-way switching at either end by each door edge,
And family members came to admire our modern room.

Rewiring done, he turned to plumbing!
The large sink in our small kitchen overbearing,
So, into the very small pantry next door it was sent,
Holes were knocked out, pipes cut and bent.

Mother urging "call the plumber out"
Father ignoring her frantic shout.
Two pipes to connect, but no jointing gear,
Solved with length of cycle inner tube, lying just near.

Connection done, water turned on and began to flow
Through the system, out of the tap and away, not slow.
Tap turned off, the pressure built as there we stood,
The tyre tube ballooned, bang! we had a flood.

Those two lessons have stayed with me all my life,
Weekend DIY, you'll need a part, or a handy wife.
Leave house plumbing to those who know,
With the special joint, or a torch to blow.

Mother wanted him to hear the Government's plead,
Train to be a teacher and fill the peacetime need.
He had no incline for such a career, I know not why,
For public speaking, he was not shy.

He picked up where he had left before,
Coaches, lorries and for a government store.
One healthy spell delivering animal food to farms,
Opening and closing gates to drop his bags in barns.

Narrow lanes, awkward corners, took toll on the front wings,
Those wheel arch covers were replaced by rubber mouldings.
Many a farmer had a fright leaning on them for some respite,
Journeys over the Clwydian hills offered him wonderful sight.

He retired after managing a water softening plant,
Water from the nearby river was softened, and sent
To the pit head a mile away, day in day out,
An independent man's job, just like driving about.

A children's Christmas party had been arranged,
Usual event at that time, nothing strange.
As church warden he was ready to go
Down to the church in deep, deep, snow.

A heater was needed, the church hall was cold,
The hall, some distance, 200 yards I am told.
He carried a heater from church to hall through snow,
Collapsing at the door, life gone, a terrible blow.

Looking back, my father was a singular man,
Happy in his own company, a Wrexham FC fan.
A small sherry was his tipple, just one, no more.
Introverted, organiser, intelligent,
but his opportunities were poor.

A man who lived through times of oppression,
WW1, 1918 epidemic, and the great depression,
WW2, many more conflicts and nuclear threats,
Fought for peace but through life I'm sure he had regrets
Chances thwarted, opportunities blocked time and again,
Had ideas and dreams, those shattered, causing pain.
His potential foiled at every turn; his talents restrained.
A husband and father unable to say
"Good-bye, hope to see you all again."

Winston Parsonage Davies   1909 - 1979

....

The final poem
is one written by my father
whilst serving in the Royal Air Force,
stationed on the Assam Burma Front.

'KINGSWAY'

By S.A.C. W P Davies

No. 4 BASE SIGNALS DEPOT, A.C.S.E.A.

THE EXPERIENCE OF ONE TRYING FAITHFULLY
TO SERVE HIS GOD, KING AND COUNTRY
ON THE ASSAM BURMA FRONT

THE GOLDEN GATE

In far off India's continent,
It fell my lot to roam,
Among a clime and people
Quite different from home.
Their creeds, their casts, and customs,
With language varied too,
Made interesting study,
A travel strange, yet true.

Way out upon the mountains,
Among a tribal race,
The almost strange surroundings
Made one feel out of place.
Oh! how I longed for England,
For home and loved ones dear,
A Sabbath morn, the waving corn,
And Church bells ringing clear

One day while travelling northwards,
Along a mountain track,
We came upon two tribesmen,
With loads upon their back.
With guttural sounds and wavings,
They made us understand,
That both begged to be given
A lift across the land.

Although it was not the custom,
We nodded our assent,
For a kindness shown to hill folk,
Is a kindness only lent;
With evident grins of pleasure,
They tumbled in behind,
As o'er the rocky pathway
Our little truck did wind.

And then, to our amazement,
They burst forth into song,
Although the words I knew not,
To join my heart did long.
For the tunes that they were singing
Came floating through the air,
'Onward Christian Soldiers',
'When the roll's called I'll be there'.

They spoke no words of English,
But presently we learned,
That they from heathen practice
To Christ himself had turned.
For, to their hillside village
A missionary came,
And brought the joyful tidings
Of that dear precious name.

Again, while climbing, upwards,
Before a coolie band,
I felt the King of Glory
Come shake me by the hand.
For the foremost of my bearers
Asked me in English new,
'Are you a Christian Sahib?
Me Jesu Christian too'.

And once, while busy cooking
As we prepared for food,
There came sweet maiden voices
From out the jungle wood.
We looked at one another,
Amazement plain to see
For the songs they sang were English,
'Tipperary' and 'Capri'.

I crept a little closer,
To spy four gathering wood,
So asked them quite politely
How come they understood
The songs they had been singing
In language strange yet plain,
And if they would but only
Repeat them once again.

The eldest of the maidens
Then answered with a smile,
We, English learn at mission
And have done for a while.
And so, with gentle pleading
I learned beyond the hill
There stood a tiny mission
Where enter all who will.

The following Sabbath evening
I thought that I would take
Myself unto that mission
And worship for his sake.
The place seemed bare and barren,
One oil lamp lit the gloom,
But I felt when o'er the threshold
His presence in the room.

The lesson of the evening
In language strange was read.
I next will read in English
The native preacher said.
And from each being present
Arose glad hymns of praise,
As to the King of Glory
Their hearts and voice did raise.

And now, announced the preacher
The choir for us will sing,
And through those thatch-filled arches
An anthem loud did ring.
The words were clear as crystal
As o'er the night air late
Came the question, 'Are you ready
To enter the Golden Gate?'

I gazed upon their numbers,
All cloaked in gaudy dress,
Bangles, rings, and ornaments
Intended to impress.
No shoes upon their feet they wore,
No covering for their hair,
'Sinner', came the pleading call
'Are you ready to enter there?'

My mind went back to childhood,
To days that I had spent
A'listening to the speaker,
Describing how we sent
Each year, to far off countries
Our pennies for to teach
Those little coloured children
The love of Christ for each.

I thought of countless efforts
Of gifts, and time thus given
To swell those funds so needed
To guide new souls to heaven.
And now those very efforts
Were gathering up fresh weight,
'Are you ready?' came the challenge
'To enter the Golden Gate'.

I slowly left that sacred scene
And homeward made my way,
Towards the little compound
Where we had chanced to stay.
My heart was full of sunshine
The brightest to relate,
For before me shone a vision
Of that future Golden Gate.

That night, within my humble tent,
I bowed my head in prayer
'God bless my home and loved ones
Keep them safe beneath thy care'.
And then I cried in accents wild,
'Oh! let this be my fate,
Lord help me meet that NAGA CHOIR
Within THE GOLDEN GATE.

Older men declare war.
But it is the youth that must fight and die.

Herbert Hoover